TO MY PARENTS
*for raising me to believe that
anything is possible*

TO MY HUSBAND AND MY CHILDREN
for making everything possible

Tom,
A GREAT SUBJECT THESE
DAYS... HOPE YOU ENJOY
THS READ.
MERRY CHRISTMAS !

Glenn

THE POWER
OF
TRUST

How Top Companies Build,
Manage And Protect It

NATALIE DOYLE OLDFIELD

CONTENTS

Acknowledgements

Prologue: Trust in Crisis   *i*

Introduction: Why Trust?   *v*

1 Your Hidden Asset: Discover the Power of a Trust-Based Business   1

Case Study – Trust Restored: The British Royal Family   **16**

2 The Science and the Evidence: How we all make Critical Trust Decisions   25

3 First impressions: We Trust What We Believe, See and Experience   47

4 Becoming a Trusted Advisor   61

Case Study – Meet a Trust Leader: Scotiabank   **76**

5 How Leaders Buid Trust: The Eight Principles of Building, Strengthening
   and Protecting Trust   85

   1. Listen Carefully with Empathy and Compassion, Question and Involve   87

   2. Communicate using Clear, Concrete and Conversational Language   107

   3. Be Honest and Transparent   121

   4. Be Consistent, Predictable and Reliable   135

   5. Act in the Best Interests of Customers, Stakeholders and the Public   153

   6. Do the Right Thing. If you Make a Mistake, Fix it   165

   7. Deliver on your Promise   177

   8. Commit to the Long Term   189

Case Study – A Century of Trust: the Key to IBM's Success   **198**

6 Protecting your Trust Equity   205

7 Building Trust in the Online Minefield   233

Case Study – eBay's Trust Model in the Online World   **244**

8 Communicating Trust To the Public Audience: This is not PR   249

9 Red Flags: Identifying your Critical Trust Risk Points   261

10 When Trust Fails: Creating a Trust Crisis Response Strategy   273

Case Study – Regaining Trust After a Crisis: Maple Leaf Foods   **278**

Conclusion: You Have to Earn Trust   293

Index   *297*

Acknowledgements

This book would not have been possible without the support and contributions of many friends, colleagues and family members. I want to thank them for sticking with me and my passion for the subject of Trust.

Firstly, I wish to thank my father, Arthur Doyle, who inspired me to write this book. As the project went on, he and I became more and more excited about Trust. I will always be grateful for his insights, edits, daily follow-ups, debates, questioning and encouragement to "do another draft, then call me." His enthusiasm has never wavered. My mother, Bonnie Doyle, was instrumental to the success of this book as she gave us ideas and put up with the daily calls and the banter from the two of us.

I would like to make a special note of my research mentor, thesis advisor and colleague, Dr. Alla Kushniryk, Department of Communication Studies, Mount Saint Vincent University. I am grateful to Alla for her guidance, expertise and patience. Alla played a singular role, sticking with me each step of the way. Getting the right research team members on board was the most important factor. This research would not have been possible without her.

To Dr. Cindy Forbes, John Feeley and Jennifer Arnold and the entire research team at the Canadian Medical Association; to my brother Arthur Doyle for his advice in the final stages of the research process, to Dr. Binod Sundararajan, Rowe School of Business, Dalhousie University for his invaluable advice and ability to put anything onto a graph or into a formula; to Alyssa Simon, an outstanding graduate student and researcher at Mount Saint Vincent University who crunched numbers, managed SPSS and formulas, and added her scientific and quantitative insights.

I was very fortunate to have the participation of executives who patiently answered my questions and shared their experiences and perspectives during long and detailed in-depth interviews and sometimes multiple follow-up conversations.

To each of the following people, I am thankful: Greg Agvent, David Alston, Mary Dable Arab, Brian Bieron, Bill Brydon, Lisa Burke, Ted Bravakis, Dennis Campbell, Ian Cavanagh, Pierre Cléroux, Richard Edelman, Frank Eliason, John Fountain, Darell Fowlie, Susan Helstab, Jamie Irving, Dr. May Gao, Dr. James Grunig, Scott McCain, Jim McGee, David Phillips, Dean Robertson, Michael Scott, Heather Tulk, and Richard Wagner.

I would also like to acknowledge the following organizations and companies for their participation: CNN, Bird Construction, BravaComm, Bank of America, Introhive, Scotiabank, Ambassatours GrayLine, E&Y, eBay, Edelman, BDC, Citicorp, Four Seasons Hotels and Resorts, Huawei Technologies, Irving, Kohltech Windows and Entrance Systems, Maple Leaf Foods, The Shaw Group, Precision BioLogic, Bell Canada, Acadian Seaplants, Marriott Hotels and IBM.

I owe a special debt of appreciation to Barbara Brooks Kimmel at Trust Across America for her pioneering work in the field of organization trust and for sharing her perspectives on trust. To Paul Niven, author of The Balanced Score Card Step by Step and Objectives and Key Results, for his extensive research and writing and for generously sharing his time.

To the many researchers and professionals in the field of organizational trust whose work I reference throughout the book, I am grateful.

I am particularly indebted to my talented editors. From the very first editor of my academic papers, my sister Bonnie Doyle Creber, who challenged me to explain theories in simple everyday language; to my sister Nancy Champion who with a pen can "clean up" any sentence; and to my sister Heather Doyle Landry, who shares trust issues and trust stories on a continual basis; and to Cathy Little for being the chief designer. I am especially grateful to Derek Flynn, for listening, for his insights, reading, editing and for the generosity with his time.

I am grateful to Lori McKay and to John Leahy for introducing us. Lori questioned, commented and edited the first draft of the manuscript and months later proof read the final manuscript. Without Lori, this book would not have been possible.

I feel most fortunate to have had a prize-winning journalist, editor and author, Dan Leger, apply his 'magic' and his exacting edits to this manuscript. I appreciate his guidance and diligence in ensuring we had the most current data, and for his wisdom.

I am especially grateful to my chief editor and reader, my father, who edited hundreds if not thousands of pages with the same enthusiasm and spark as if it was the first page. For as long as I can remember, he has shared his experiences and wisdom with me. Every page bears his imprint.

To my clients, many of whom inspire me every single day, thank you. I am especially grateful to them for sharing their customer stories and trust issues with me.

To all these and many others who have helped in one way or another, I am grateful. The responsibility for any shortcomings and errors the book may have is, of course, entirely my own.

Lastly I am deeply thankful to my children, Patrick and Courtney, and my husband, Michael, who have enthusiastically believed in and supported this book and this research project that lasted almost six years. Not only is Michael my advisor, he is in my deepest and most enduring supporter.

PROLOGUE

Trust in Crisis

In the summer of 2008, public health inspectors in Ontario, Canada, started to notice an unusual number of cases of listeriosis, a bacterial infection that can lead to serious illness and even death, in patients with compromised immunity.

Listeriosis is almost always contracted from contaminated foods. Elderly people, pregnant women, newborns and others with immune system vulnerabilities are most at risk. But it's not unusual and some cases are reported in North America every year.

Caused by the bacterium Listeria monocytogenes, Listeria can cause gastroenteritis even in healthy people, who experience it as diarrhea and fever. But if not detected and treated promptly, it can stimulate deadly infections of the central nervous system in vulnerable patients.

Listeria is a common form of bacteria. It's all around us and the medical community expects to treat a number of cases of listeriosis infection every year. But what was going on in Ontario that summer seemed unusual.

The province, Canada's largest with a population of about 13 million, usually gets four to five cases a month. In June, 2008, eight cases were reported. Health authorities noticed, but weren't sure if it was a sign of trouble or just a random bump in the statistics.

In mid-July, Toronto Public Health discovered a case of listeriosis in a nursing home for the elderly. This did set off alarms and investigators were sent to the facility to take samples of the food. The samples they collected were sent to Health Canada's specialized laboratories in Winnipeg, Manitoba.

Authorities were worried, but still weren't ready to describe the spurt in listeriosis cases in Ontario as an outbreak. They first needed to confirm the presence of clusters of the same bacteria. That would require sophisticated testing and it would take time.

On August 5, Health Canada announced it had confirmed listeria contamination in a sandwich from a private nursing home in Toronto. The next day the Canadian Food Inspection Agency, the federal organization responsible for food safety, was called in.

A week later, an executive at Maple Leaf Foods took a disturbing telephone call from the Agency. A formal investigation was under way into Maple Leaf's products.

Suspicion centred on samples from a Leisureworld Senior Care Corp. nursing home and two from Joseph Brant Hospital. Investigators finally concluded that the products probably all originated from production lines 8 and 9 in Maple Leaf's Bartor Road plant. The product was marketed under the Sure Slice brand.

The company immediately complied with a request not to ship any more of the products, which were recalled across Canada.

Maple Leaf Foods, a national supplier of everything from bread to deli meat, was entering a nightmare scenario, one that few companies ever expect to confront. People were getting sick and it was because of one of their products.

The company went into emergency recall mode, pulling back all 220 products produced at its plant on Bartor Road in Toronto's Downsview suburb. Since Maple Leaf supplied the meat for dozens of other branded products, a massive sweep of all foods that had gone through the Bartor Road plant began.

But the news kept getting worse. People started dying. By August 26, the Public Health Authority of Canada said 15 people had died in Ontario, Saskatchewan and Quebec. Dozens of others were infected, with the outbreak eventually reaching seven provinces.

By the time all the evidence was in, 22 deaths had been linked to the listeriosis outbreak and all were blamed on contaminated products from one of Canada's most respected brands, Maple Leaf Foods.

On August 23, with no doubt remaining as to responsibility for the outbreak, Maple Leaf's chief executive, Michael McCain, called a news conference at the corporate headquarters in Toronto.

Everything was on the line that day for McCain and for Maple Leaf. Mishandling the response to the Listeria outbreak could destroy trust in the company's reputation for high quality, safe food products.

How McCain handled the trust issue and Maple Leaf's corporate reputation would become a textbook example of crisis management and corporate responsibility. It became a trial by fire of public trust in a company that provided products to almost every home in Canada.

McCain would be asking consumers to take what he later called "a leap of faith" in Maple Leaf's brand. It would become for Maple Leaf, its 24,000 employees and their shareholders, a matter of trust.

INTRODUCTION

Why Trust?

What is the most critical asset in your organization? Is it your product line, the service you offer, your brand identity, your staff, management team or sales organization? What singular factor can make or break your firm, your agency or organization?

The military describes a factor it calls the "centre of gravity" of any army, state or alliance. It is the critical and essential pivot for everything else that happens. A threat to the centre of gravity is existential, potentially fatal.

But what if the most critical asset isn't found in the staff directory, the executive suite or on the production line? What if it's something we all understand, yet sometimes struggle to describe? What if that critical asset is trust, just good old-fashioned trust, universally understood around the world, in every culture. It can not and must not be taken for granted. Without your customers' trust, you cease to exist. Customers buy from companies they trust, do business with companies they trust and are loyal to companies they trust. Your ability to build trust has a profound impact on your results.

Trust, therefore, is a leadership imperative. It is something for which every member of the organization is responsible. It might start at the top, but it can't end there. Smart companies know that it drives and sustains business. They also know trust is fragile, reciprocal and powerful. It takes time to build, but can be destroyed in an inattentive moment.

Every human relationship is unique but trust is the common denominator of all of them; trust in personal relationships, within families, within organizations and communities. Trust underlies all social interactions, regardless of the type of relationship or whether it's online or face-to-face, one-on-one or among organizations. Trust is essential for individuals to bond and for relationships to stabilize and develop. It cements the foundations on which they can grow. Trust is the bedrock of positive relationships. Lack of trust is at the root of many bad ones.

Trust is tangible. It is an economic driver for every organization. Measures of customer trust should be on the balance sheet of every business. Why? Because it is a key indicator of a company's future success or potential failure. In fact, a customer's trust is the most important asset a company can have, as we have seen in the many instances where companies have suffered the consequences of broken trust with customers, stakeholders or suppliers. In my years of research on trust, I looked for ways a company could measure trustworthiness, because as management expert Peter Drucker taught us "what gets measured gets managed."

My research led me to conceive and develop The Building and Protecting Trust Model and The Client Trust Index™, trademarked assessment tools that incorporate the scientific dimensions of trust, along with the behaviours and criteria that individuals use to determine if they trust an organization. It started as my graduate research, and after four years of development, the Client Trust Index™ has become a new performance metric. It is a tool that allows executives to recognize the significance of trust to their business's success. And as you will see in the following pages, trust can be measured, it can be managed and it is an indicator of future success.

When I teach executive seminars on trust, I ask participants to describe what it feels like when their customers lose trust in them. The most frequent descriptors include: challenging, uncomfortable, awkward and stressful. When I ask "What happens to the business?'" the most common answers are declining revenues, lack of repeat business, decline in the number of referrals, difficulty in recruiting new employees and in establishing partnership opportunities. The research backs up what my customers have shared with me in seminars.

Companies and organizations will acknowledge that trust is an important asset, yet many ignore the threats to their "trust equity" until it becomes a crisis. Most CEOs do not have a plan to strengthen and protect their trust brand or their trust equity. It is rare to hear a company president even mention the term trust in a speech, blog post or annual report. The concept of building a "trust culture" is rarely on their agenda. It almost seems that CEOs especially, feel that the corporate reputation reflects directly on their ethics and their reputation. To even suggest there is anything like a trust issue in play might suggest there's some underlying problem at the top.

This is a dangerous omission. Companies that fail to nurture a culture of trust risk harsh consequences if that trust disappears. Some, such as the Volkswagen Group in its emissions scandal, are learning that the hard way. Volkswagen's trust failure, rigging 11 million diesels with software to evade emissions standards, cost the company billions of dollars. United Airlines became an unwilling Internet sensation in 2017 when it overbooked a flight and called in security staff to eject a passenger declared surplus. Video of the man being dragged off the plane became a YouTube sensation. It cost United Airlines millions of dollars, its share price was shredded and the ruckus caused a crisis in airline customer relations.

Even the smallest organizations rely on tiny acts of trust. Codes of conduct, human resources policies and organizational processes and procedures encourage good behavior. However, some organizations do not have formal human resources policies and few have the personnel to 'police' everyone to 'be good' all the time. Trust keeps an organization running. Just turning on your laptop requires faith that the IT department is looking after the network, that the organization will not abuse the customer's private credit card information or the employee's confidential information. More complex organizations and companies require much higher degrees of trust.

Trust in an organization is not a frill; it is essential. As former U.S. Secretary of State Colin Powell said, "Trust is the glue that holds an organization together and the lubricant that keeps it moving forward." Cultivating trust is difficult. It takes time, deliberate effort and commitment. Yet trust is also fragile and can be lost in an instant.

THE BUSINESS CASE FOR TRUST

Companies that operate with integrity and trust outperform. Trust Across America tracks the performance of America's most trustworthy public companies. They have found that the most trustworthy companies outperform the S&P 500. Trust Across America's Corporate Integrity Monitor is the most comprehensive and fact-based ongoing study on the subject of corporate trustworthiness and integrity. Since 2008 it has measured the corporate trustworthiness and integrity of the largest 2000 US public companies.

During the three-year period from February 2013-February 2016, and according to Trust Across America's proprietary FACTS® Framework, America's most trustworthy public companies outperformed the Standard and Poor (S&P) 500 by 1.8x. The composite results translate to 16.7 per cent.

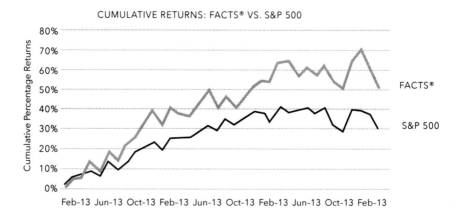

Reprinted with permission of Trust Across America

The Great Place to Work and Fortune Magazine publish the "100 Best Compa-nies to Work For" in which trust comprises sixty percent of the criteria, since their research shows that "trust between managers and employees is the primary defining characteristic of the very best workplaces." These companies beat "the average annu-alized returns of the S&P 500 by a factor of three."

Interaction Associates reported that high-trust companies "are more than two and a half times more likely to be high performing revenue organizations" than low-trust companies in 2015.

The Edelman Trust Barometer, the largest macro study on trust worldwide, summarized its 2017 findings as "Trust in Crisis." Trust in government, media, non-government organizations and business has declined significantly since 2012. Trust in the media is at an all-time low, with a distrust rating of 82 per cent. Glob-ally, Edelman determined that "Business is on the Brink of Distrust," with only 52 per cent trusting corporations to do what is right.

This book will offer practical strategies, tips and stories of how leading compa-nies manage trust. I will share with you how you can measure trust in your busi-ness. We will review the science and the evidence behind trust and look at how that critical decision to trust, or not, is made by customers and stakeholders.

We will also examine how leaders build trust through Eight Principles that build, strengthen and protect trust. We'll cover best practices for applying the prin-ciples to the way you do business. I'll make observations and offer suggestions of how to apply them and I'll present examples of how companies and professionals can apply the principles.

We will also look at red flags, how to identify and remove them and common mistakes companies make with their customers. We will offer practical to-dos and don't evers, that you can start applying right away. And while I do offer advice about deploying trust as the best asset in your inventory, this isn't really an advice book. Every organization is different and there's no single recipe to build, strengthen or protect relationships of trust.

I believe that organizations should start with data, facts and research. Consider this book your starting point to building and protecting trust with customers, and creating a stronger business because of it.

Some of the organizations cited in this book, and the people associated with them, have probably made mistakes and may do so again. Organizations are not perfect any more than people are.

The examples in this book give us lessons on how trust is built or damaged. It is important to focus on your own situation and take the lessons that apply.

Trust: a firm belief in the reliability, truth, ability or strength of someone or something - Oxford Dictionary

Synonyms for trust include confidence, belief, faith, certainty, assurance, conviction, credence and reliance - Oxford Dictionary

As Charles Duhigg reported in The New York Times, Google studied a 180 teams to determine how to build the perfect team. The research, called Project Aristotle, found the key ingredient and the strongest predictor of high performing teams is built on a culture of trust.

1

Your Hidden Asset: Discover the Power of a Trust-Based Business

When I conduct seminars with companies, I often ask participants to name a company or two they are loyal and committed to, or a business with such a good reputation they would pay more for its products or services. The list that emerges usually has a few local companies I'm not familiar with, but it also includes some well-known larger companies.

One name that often comes up is WestJet, an employee-owned Canadian airline based in Alberta. Not surprisingly, in May 2017 it was named one of Canada's top 10 most trusted brands and Canada's most trusted airline, according to the Gustavson Brand Trust Index. WestJet was inducted into the corporate culture hall of fame after being named one of Canada's Most Admired Corporate Cultures in 2005, 2006, 2007 and 2008.

When I ask participants why they admire WestJet, the responses include "The people are friendly," "They make me feel important," "Employees want to help," "The service is outstanding," and "They care about their customers and the communities." In May 2017, WestJet laid out the four pillars of success as key parts of its corporate strategic plan. Number one of the four pillars is 'People and Culture' including WestJet's commitment to its people. 'Guest Experience' is the second pillar.

WestJet goes above and beyond for its customers and the company supports local communities. In 2016, WestJet sent planes to Fort McMurray, Alberta, to rescue people from one of Canada's most devastating forest fires. WestJet executives and staffers put themselves in their customer's shoes and showed them how much they care. Sometimes it's the little things that make a difference with big companies. WestJet has documented some of these stories on their Youtube channel. You can watch the stories of WestJetters, which is what the employees call themselves, bringing families together when someone is sick, for example, or by flying people across the country for Father's Day.

WestJet employees are owners. Therefore, employees have an "owner mentality" because they share in the company's success and dread its potential failures. As a WestJet fact sheet says, that makes a difference "Because owners care." As owners, the employees are tangibly invested in the company. Anyone with children knows firsthand what this means. When a child buys something with their own money, that item takes on a much different measure of attachment than if someone had simply bought it for them. Children will often take better care of items they pay for themselves, whether it's a $40 phone case or a $10 T-shirt. It is theirs.

> Organizations that nurture a culture of trust enjoy a hidden asset: engaged, empowered employees.

Employees who trust each other and trust the company outperform employees who don't have those relationships in their workplace. When it truly takes hold, trust improves productivity, engagement and innovation. Customers and external stakeholders notice. Distrust inside an organization can only be buried so deeply, it always seeps out to customers.

Trust impacts everything in the corporate or organizational universe: from quality and implementation of decisions, to reputation, credibility and commitment to customers. How products or services are delivered depends on how much the leaders and employees trust each other. Therefore trust is a leadership imperative. If employees don't feel they can confidently rely on the organization to do the right thing, customers will sense this. My sister, for example, refuses to do business with a particular company because she believes its employees are kept in the dark, are treated poorly and don't trust the management. This kind of thinking is common for many people. In contrast to that firm, companies that embed a culture of trust enjoy a competitive advantage over their rivals. That is why employees are an invaluable part of uncovering your hidden asset. They are crucial to the trust equation.

Many successful organizations cite trust as a core value. They know the best outcomes are achieved when people work together, when employees are engaged, and when there is a supporting culture of trust.

Multiple studies have shown relationships between a high trust environment and improved productivity, innovation and employee engagement. Intuitively this makes sense.

Several studies show how trust benefits organizations. In a study of 355 college basketball players from 30 teams, Kurt Dirks found that members' trust in leadership positively affects the team's performance. Teams that trusted their coach won more games than the teams that did not trust their coach. The study suggests one of the reasons such performance momentum can be sustained is "because performance affects the team's trust in its leader, which in turn affects team performance." Dirks argues that this research applies in many other settings.

James Davis of University of Notre Dame, David Schoorman of Purdue University, Roger Mayer of Baylor University and Hwee Hoon Tan of National Univeristy of Sinapore study of restaurant staff and managers also demonstrates that trust in leadership is a significant determinant of a firm's financial performance, specifically sales, profit, and employee turnover rates.

In a survey of 4,200 supervisors, Professor of Management (Emeritus) Dale Zand of New York University concluded that high trust relationships stimulate higher performance. A trusting environment has a positive impact on managerial problem solving effectiveness and allows employees to have influence on decisions, which results in more satisfied, more motivated, and more committed workers. According to Edelman, organizations with higher trust have longer-lasting relationships with their stakeholders.

Since Zand's study, several scholars have written about strong employee commitment in organizations with cultures high in trust, including Gilbert Fairholm, Adjunct Professor of Management Systems at the University of Richmond and Professor Robert Hurley, of Fordham University.

Low trust organizations waste time and money, and create toxic work environments. Instead of getting their work done, employees end up spending valuable time trying to figure out who they can count on, who they can confide in, who really "has their back" and protecting themselves from those they can't trust.

EARNING LOYALTY, THE COSTCO EXAMPLE

Costco Wholesale (Costco) is a company that is mentioned frequently when I ask friends, customers and seminar participants to name the companies they trust. Not at all surprisingly, Costco was named one of the most trusted brands in the United States in 2011 according to Temkin Group's Trust Ratings report and one of the most trusted brands in Canada in 2016 and 2017 according to the Gustavson Brand Trust Index. Maybe we shouldn't be surprised. An executive participating in one of my seminars said her partner worked at Costco and loved it. She said "It really is an amazing company." She told our group Costco treated employees exceptionally well and her boyfriend was proud to work there.

My mother, sisters and sister-in-law are all raving fans and committed Costco shoppers. They love Costco so much that to tease them, I call it a cult. People actually pay money to shop at Costco, in fact Costco shoppers are members. Yes, members. Not customers, although they are that too by our definition. But what's significant is that members are part of an organization, something people find meaningful. I confess that I too have a Costco card.

From my perspective as a member and a shopper, Costco employees are the company's hidden asset.

> When employees trust a company, it shows up on the bottom line.

Harvard Business Review reported in an article entitled The High Cost of Low Wages, that the annual cost of Costco employee churn is $244 million versus the cost at bargain rival Sam's Club, of $612 million. We all know there are many reasons people leave companies, but a high rate of employee turnover is an indicator that employees don't trust the company. A significantly low turnover rate (five per cent in the retail industry) is an indicator of high employee trust.

Costco delivers on the promise of low price, high-quality merchandise. From what I have experienced, I bet if we conducted the Client Trust Index™ on Costco, customers would rate the company exceptionally high, perhaps in the 90 – 100 per cent on the Client Trust Index™ continuum.

HOW DO YOU BUILD A CULTURE OF TRUST?

When there's a culture of trust inside an organization, customers know. There are lots of signs: employees speak well of the company, they are proud and engaged. If people are not proud of where they work or if they don't trust their employer, how can someone ask or expect customers to trust them?

It is often said that the best sales people really believe in their products, offerings and their companies. It just makes sense. If you really believe the product is outstanding and it is the right thing for the customer, then the customer is going to feel that sincerity. Conversely, if you work for an organization and the organization says the product is amazing but you as the sales person know it doesn't perform as advertised, it will come across to the customer.

When you go to a coffee shop and the person serving you is disengaged, preoccupied or not happy with fellow employees, it's obvious. They don't ask if you want a cookie or biscuit with the coffee, they don't ask if there's anything else you would like, they don't tell you about the newest promotion, and they typically do not thank you. Building trust with customers starts with making a connection. Typically, we do not connect with people who are disengaged because it is clear that they just don't care.

A company's hidden asset truly is a culture of trust in the organization, where employees trust the leaders and the company. As former IBM CEO Lou Gerstner said in his book Who Says Elephants Can't Dance? Inside IBM's Historic Turnaround, "I came to see in my time at IBM that culture isn't just one aspect of the game — it is the game."

When you apply the Eight Principles of Building, Protecting and Strengthening Trust within an organization, a culture of trust builds and percolates inside the organization, and it shows itself in customer interactions. Companies need to work on both building a culture of trust internally and with the customers.

Building that trust culture starts at the top with the leader and the leadership team. Barbara Brooks Kimmel, executive director of Trust Across America - Trust Around the World, is quoted saying, "Remember, the fish rots from the head. Every problem in every organization, including low trust, can be traced back to its leadership."

Once a culture of trust is in place with the leadership team, the next job is aligning employees. When employee values are closely aligned with the organization's values, everyone is working together to achieve the same goal and the organization performs at a higher level. Everyone in a company needs to know what is expected of them. What is their purpose in the organization? What role do they play in achieving the organization's goals?

You can look at an organizational culture as a pattern of beliefs, shared values, and assumptions that are looked at as the appropriate way to think and act within that company. Culture is often defined as "The way we do things around here." A corporate culture of trust is fundamental to building and protecting trust with customers.

Define your corporate culture by answering the following questions:

1. What are the current core values and beliefs of the organization?
2. What values and beliefs guide our daily interactions?
3. What are we really committed to?

WHAT IS A CUSTOMER CENTERED TRUST CULTURE?

Simply put, it is a culture in which employees are acting in the customer's best interest. It is a culture where everyone in the organization knows what the goals and objectives are, one where everyone is singing off the same song sheet and rowing in the same direction. It is an organization where everyone from the receptionist to the person in the corner office is focused on building and strengthening relationships with customers, partners, stakeholders and colleagues. One where employees put the customers' interests ahead of strick adherence to job descriptions. It is an organization where everyone knows they have a part to play in impacting the customer's decision to trust the company. When customers trust the company and its employees, they are saying 'yes' to the company, its ideas, products and services.

HOW DO WE KNOW WHEN A COMPANY HAS A CUSTOMER CENTERED TRUST CULTURE?

- Employees give off positive vibes. Their attitude and mindset is focused on the customer. They talk about their customers' successes and are proud of them
- Employees are engaged. They embrace their role and know how and what they do affects customers
- Everyone in the company says the same things about the company and what it does. Employees understand the purpose, their role and how it impacts the customer
- Employees answer questions confidently and consistently
- The company has strong and often longstanding relationships with customers, partners and suppliers, and is committed to these relationships long term
- They go out of their way to seek feedback from customers
- Employees understand what it means to act in the customer's best interests and are empowered to do so

SIX STEPS TO INSTILL A CUSTOMER CENTERED TRUST CULTURE

1. Establish a code of conduct and company values. Once established, everyone from the president to the newest employee needs to know what they are, and work by that code and those values.

2. Understand your customer's experience with your company. See yourself through your customers' eyes. What is it really like to deal with your company? Are there areas for improvements or processes that would make it easier for the customer to do business with you?

3. Gain a full understanding of your customers and their world. What is a day in the life like for them?

4. Follow The Eight Principles of Building, Strengthening and Protecting Trust with colleagues and customers.

5. Align organizational processes; roles and performance objectives with your customer trust building strategy.

6. Measure every employee's performance as it relates to his or her trust strengthening behaviours, communications and how they serve customers. The commitment should be to continuous improvement over the long term

A customer centered trust culture is one where employees are empowered to think differently, and to make decisions that affect the customers' best interests, without having to go through hoops or continually check with management.

Employers need to ask: Is every employee currently focused on building trust with customers? Does every employee focus on the particular needs of each customer? Are your employees empowered to service the customer's best interests?

Organizations that are purpose - led outperform

Simon Sinek, author of the book, "Start with Why," encourages people to feel inspired and inspire others. He asks, "Do you know your Why? The purpose, cause, or belief that inspires you to do what you do?" Purpose-led companies, where employees, systems and processes are aligned, generally outperform. When everyone understands the organization's purpose and everyone is working towards the same goal, spectacular things can happen.

Weight Watchers has a single goal: to help its customers lose weight. Every employee of Weight Watchers is expected to have that goal as their prime focus, no matter what their role is in the company. There are countless examples in business of companies and employees who have performed miracles, solved challenges and created new opportunities, almost all of them identified the mission and got everyone focused on that.

An EY Beacon Institute and Harvard Business Review study reported that 90 per cent of executives believe purpose matters. Companies with a strong sense of purpose outperform.

DISNEY: In trusted organizations, every single employee — no matter what they do – understands their purpose. At Disney, for example, every employee understands they are about making magical moments for their guests. Employees are referred to as "cast members." Whether they are a photographer in a theme park or a clerk in a retail store, everyone is well versed in the most common questions the guests ask, simple queries like "Where is the washroom?" "What time is the parade?" and "Where is the parade?" Employees are taught to be empathetic with their guests and to anticipate what the guest is really asking. Employees are ready with their responses: "The closest washroom is there," "The parade starts are 3 p.m. and if you stand right here it will go by you at 3:20 p.m." "If you stand there, the tree will give you shade and if you take a picture from there the castle will be in the background." Responses like these are how Disney creates a magical experience for guests. When everyone in the organization knows the purpose, everyone can deliver on the promise. When there is clarity and simplicity around the vision, purpose and promise, employees are empowered to act in the customer's best interests and to wow them. Employees are Disney's hidden asset.

GOOGLE: In the book, How Google Works, Eric Schmidt and Jonathan Rosenberg discuss the Google culture. How things work at Google is their hidden asset. In their book, Schmidt and Rosenberg defined Google as one of the world's most successful companies. They say their values are honesty, transparency, innovation, communication and performance. The former CEO and COO describe the culture of transparency in detail and define how it is operationalized, from the specific activities and Objectives Key Results (OKR) to policies and how employees, referred to as Googlers, are made accountable.

As with most successful companies, it is best practice to start with a vision and clear objectives. Google clearly operationalizes this as part of their culture, as everyone in the organization – including the founders – has an outline for their individual objectives and strategic goals. Everything is in line with the company's vision and its strategic goals. Employees post their OKR on the company "MOMA" intranet system for all to see. This promotes communication, transparency and indicated how each individual is delivering on the company promise. OKRs are reported on and updated on a regular basis. All employees, regardless of position, are required to post updates quarterly. This provides a quick, easy and efficient way to view what others' priorities are and what they are working on. Employees provide weekly updates by posting snippets. Snippets are weekly updates where employees post the most important things they are working on to MOMA. This way, executives can always see what's going on and a culture of transparent, concrete communication is fostered. As described by Schmidt and Rosenberg, these policies and codes of conduct are enforced, and decisions are made to support the company values. When employees break company confidences, for example by forwarding email outside of the company, they are fired. Trust is enhanced when companies have clear policies and everyone is treated the same.

Further, Google executives conduct weekly employee question and answer sessions to stay engaged with employees. Google refers to them as TGIF sessions. Employees submit questions via MOMA and then vote on the importance of the question and management's response to them.

In 2014, the Edelman Trust Barometer examined specific actions CEOs can take to build trust and the level of importance of these actions to the general public. Eighty per cent of respondents of the Edelman Trust Barometer reported that when the CEO engages regularly with employees, it creates trust.

CNN: CNN is a trust leader and an example of a company that is clear on its vision, its values and its objectives. I spoke to Greg Agvent, senior director of news operations at CNN, who described the core value of the CNN brand as all about truth and trust. "Seeking truth in an unambiguous and unfiltered way. There are so many shades of grey in any story. Holding people accountable to the truth. Our brand is absolutely about trust. Without trust we have nothing." He went on to describe how CNN built a culture of trust. "It is kind of self-perpetuating. You put good people with integrity and great character together to form the team. Ted Turner started this in 1980. The people that started with the company in the early 1980s are the people in the leadership roles today. These people have integrity and great character. We have a culture of growth, honesty, and integrity when it comes to the journalism. We believe it is an honor, privilege and a responsibility to work here." It's one of the reasons for the famous CNN tag line: "the most trusted name in news."

A CULTURE OF TRUST INCREASES ENGAGEMENT
HUAWEI TECHNOLOGIES

While speaking at a conference, I met an executive from Huawei Technologies of Shenzhen, China. Huawei is one of the world's largest information and communications technology ICT companies and one of China's most trusted firms. A few interesting facts about Huawei:

+ First mainland China company to make Top 100 Best Global Brands, 2015
+ Named among Boston Consulting Group's 2015 Most Innovative Companies
+ LinkedIn recognized Huawei as one of the World's 100 Most In Demand Employers, 2014 (This is awarded to the most sought-after employees based on billions of interactions from LinkedIn 300M + members)
+ Thomson Reuters named Huawei a Top 100 Global Innovator, 2014

With operations in more than 170 countries, its 176,000 employees represent 160 nationalities. I met several Huawei employees at SAUPO (Symposium on Asia-U.S. Partnership Opportunities) and was impressed with their enthusiasm and customer focus. When I asked Jim McGee, senior director of government relations for the United States, how Huawei become one of China's most trusted brands he replied, "We are 100 per cent employee owned. Everyone in the company is focused on providing superior service to the customer and creating a connected world. We are all focused on achieving the same results for our company and our customers. We focus on developing our employees; our employees are engaged and have a deep understanding of the company vision."

Later that day, during a panel discussion, the CEO of one of Huawei's value added partners, Raymond Cheng of SoZo Solutions said, "Huawei focuses on authentic partnerships and relationships. They focus on a person-to-person level with customers."

From what I learned, it looks like Huawei is delivering on it's promise: "Commitment to Building a Better Connected World." According to a 2016 Huawei Corporate Briefing, as the third largest smart phone provider, Huawei touches one third of the world's population. It provides Internet access to more people around the world than any other company. We trust brands that deliver on their promises. In addition to its remarkable track record of delivering on its promise, Huawei's culture of trust and employee focus may just be one of its hidden assets. Be a trust leader and the key performance indicators (KPIs) will follow.

TRUST ASSESSMENT

Building a culture of trust starts with you. Before you fully launch into how to build trust with customers, ask yourself what you do to strengthen trust with your colleagues. What do you do that would undermine trust? Take time to reflect on the past six months and look ahead to your goals for the next six.

Here are eight questions that will assist you in assessing your trustworthiness:

1. Do you listen with respect, patience and genuine interest when interacting with colleagues?

2. Does your body language always communicate patience, or does it sometimes convey boredom or impatience?

3. Do you keep confidences your colleagues share with you?

4. Are you consistently on time for meetings?

5. Do you respond to calls, emails and requests in a timely manner?

6. Do you do what you say you are going to do? Or do you over-promise and under-deliver?

7. Do you demonstrate empathy and compassion for a colleague's concerns?

8. Do you share all relevant workplace information with your colleagues?

CASE STUDY

Trust Restored
The British Royal Family

The British royal family is one of the world's oldest brands–yes, brands – and arguably one of the most recognized brands in the world. For the purpose of this case study, let's establish that the definition of brand is the experience people have with an organization. The organization of the British monarchy was first established more than 1,200 years ago to rule first England, then the sprawling Empire and eventually, the Commonwealth. The current royal family, the House of Windsor, took that name in 1917.

How does the example of the British royal family fit into a business book about building trust with customers? It fits because it's a great example of an organization that lost trust with its stakeholders, in this case the British public, and regained it. Many of the largest and the most successful corporations in the world have at some point faced a decline in public or customer trust. Often this loss has resulted in a decline in sales and shareholder value and in some cases outright failure.

In the fall of 2011, while a graduate student, I wrote my first trust research paper on how the British royal family regained the public's trust through the wedding of Prince William and Catherine (Kate) Middleton. I felt it was a fitting case to share because it was also the beginning of my academic research on trust.

Public trust for the royal family eroded over a series of events from 1996 to 2005. It started to erode in 1996 with the divorce of

CASE STUDY

Prince Andrew and Sarah Ferguson; followed by the messy public divorce of Prince Charles and Lady Diana Spencer in the same year. The family's handling of Diana's death in 1997 and the subsequent marriage of Prince Charles and Camilla Parker Bowles in 2005 contributed to the erosion.

Throughout and following these events, along with reports of their activities and spending, the public began to question the relevance of the royal family. The erosion of trust often takes place over time, with a number of cumulative actions, behaviours, communications and events that become a slow leak. These royal family incidents took place over nine years, a relatively slow leak. However some might argue that for a 1,200 year-old organization, nine years is a rapid leak.

In 2010, the engagement of Prince William to Catherine Middletown presented the organization with an opportunity to rebuild the public's trust. It could reinvent and re-establish itself as relevant and trustworthy. Many organizations go through the process of re-establishing trust with stakeholders and this is an excellent example. The royal family re-established itself as relevant and cast itself once more in a favourable light. It is also an example of an organization that applied the principles of trust to achieve its goal of re-establishing public trust.

The 2011 Royal Wedding of Prince William and Catherine Middleton

Given the media coverage of the 2011 royal wedding of William and Kate, the couple and the much-anticipated event became the royal family's access point of trust to the public. As we will discuss

CASE STUDY

later, the wedding became a critical trust risk point for the organization.

Starting with the engagement, the royal family offered open access to the public and involved citizens in the event. A media interview following the engagement allowed a view into their relationship and a way to get to know them. For 17 minutes, the couple answered questions about how they met and about their wedding plans; making it easy for people to become familiar with them. Typically, the royal family does not grant access, Queen Elizabeth has never granted an interview.

William and Kate demonstrated vulnerability, showed their compassion and involved the public in their relationship by offering access to their world. For millions of people, it was the first time they heard the voices of William and Kate. They demonstrated that they were much like every other young couple in love. We trust people we know, people we can connect with and people who are like us. The interview represented a critical step toward rebuilding trust with the public and the young royals executed it well.

This access created a sense of familiarity, which is important when deciding to trust. We do not trust if we do not know. Openness is a key dimension of trust. The royal family was transparent, communicated the wedding plans with the media and invited the media to the church. The ceremony was broadcast live on television, radio, YouTube, and on large screens outside the church, where crowds gathered to watch. These actions demonstrated an effort to make ordinary Britons feel like active participants in the wedding.

The media played a significant role in rebuilding public trust for the royal family. An estimated two billion people in 180

CASE STUDY

countries watched all or part of the royal wedding according to the Telegraph newspaper. According to the 2011 Telegraph article, Royal Wedding Facts and Figures, 8,500 media journalists covered the event and more than 300 tweets per second were transmitted. The media reported on the behaviour and emotions of the couple with rigorous detail. Stories and news coverage enforced the view of the couple as trustworthy, competent, open and reliable.

The media reported that the event went off without a hitch. The British royal family delivered on its promise. Journalists and bloggers reported on Kate as sincere, authentic, confident, reliable and open. One key message of the organization was that the couple was "of the people." People trust people who are like them, and people they can relate to. Kate was portrayed as familiar and sincere, both characteristics of the behavioural dimension of trust. "She appeared slightly emotional as she repeated her vows," as quoted in NBC today. If Kate did not appear nervous, the public would not believe she was authentic. People Magazine reported that Colleen Harris, the former press secretary of Prince William said, "They're not stuffy people. They are un-pompous and open."

Being punctual, relaxed, confident and reliable demonstrate trustworthy, predictable behaviour. "On the stroke of 11 a.m. with Big Ben's chime and the abbey's own 10 bells sounding out, the bride's vintage Rolls Royce Phantom VI pulled up and the crowds went absolutely wild," was how Hello Magazine Canada described the scene. Kate was on schedule. It was reported that it took her four minutes to walk up the aisle with her father, just as scheduled.

Both traditional and social media responded positively to

CASE STUDY

the royal wedding. "It was a perfect event, but also a moment of triumph for a beleaguered royal family—and a sign of things to come," according to Maclean's Magazine. The Daily Mail, a UK based newspaper, published results of a public opinion poll on June 23, 2011, which suggested that "more than a third of Britons now feel more patriotic" since the couple wed.

Since 2011, the royal family continues to be seen in positive light. In 2012, Queen Elizabeth took part of the opening ceremonies of the London Olympics and William and Kate were treated like superstars. They have become part of popular culture, even making it to Netflix. In the fall of 2016, the Netflix series The Crown told the story of the royal family, starting in 1947.

Applying the Eight Principles of Trust to this Case:

1 **Listen carefully with empathy and compassion, question and involve the public in the conversation.** Beginning with the intimate interview following the engagement, the couple listened to the questions that were asked of them and responded. They empathized with the public and answered questions people wanted to know. They shared information about themselves and showed their vulnerabilities. Through this media interview they involved the British public in the conversation.

2 **Communicate using clear, concrete and conversational language.** The organization consistently reported on the timeline and details about the wedding day across multiple mediums. The public was kept well informed, from posting

CASE STUDY

a picture of the official engagement notice displayed outside Buckingham Palace, to publishing the map of the route the horses and carriages would take from the palace to the church.

3 **Be honest and transparent.** From the engagement announcement, to the interview, to the events leading up to the wedding itself, the royal family shared openly what was happening. Little was held back from the public. The night before the wedding, William surprised Londoners by going outside to talk to well-wishers. He was sincere and honest, telling them he was "nervous and excited."

4 **Be consistent, predictable and reliable.** The event was scheduled, timed to precision and executed perfectly. The royal family provided the pageantry, traditions and entertainment that the public expected. It was similar to other British royal weddings. There were no surprises.

5 **Act in the best interests of the customers, stakeholders and the public.** The wedding ceremony was televised for the world to see. This demonstrated the family was acting in the public's best interests.

6 **Do the right thing. If you make a mistake, fix it.** All protocols were followed, with a few minor exceptions. For example, when the bride walked up the aisle of Westminster Abbey, protocol stated she should curtsy or bow when she reached Queen Elizabeth. Kate forgot to do this. This was a mistake, one of the few that was noted. Previous royal brides have

CASE STUDY

all curtsied when entering and leaving the church. The bride corrected the mistake and curtseyed when she left Westminster Abbey.

7. **Deliver on your promise.** The royal family delivered a fairy tale wedding with suitably traditional pomp and pageantry. Etiquette Blogger William Hanson reported seeing a handmade sign in London on the day of the wedding that said, "Don't expect the Olympics to be this good."

8. **Commit to the long term.** Royal family wedding traditions were followed, and the pageantry demonstrated the family's commitment to the British people and to the royal family organization's traditions and values.

*Many of the largest and most successful
corporations and organizations in the world
have at some point experienced
a decline in customer or public trust.*

~

*William and Kate resonated with the public
as they brought authenticity, transparency
and accessibility to the organization.*

2

The Science and the Evidence: How We All Make Critical Trust Decisions

Trust is complex, complicated and it is time based. Customers decide consciously and subconsciously to trust an organization and its employees based on how it communicates, how it serves them and how it behaves. Trust is a predictor of future success.

I f you ask someone if they trust a company, they can often say yes or no, but if you were to ask them why or by how much, they probably wouldn't have a definitive answer. Intuitively, we already know a lot about trust, it is part of every interaction in our lives. We certainly know very clearly when we don't trust someone. It is obvious. Yet trust is difficult to see, to describe and to quantify. You can't touch it, hear it or smell it. But it is real.

Trust is a tangible component of all relationships. It can be measured and therefore it can be managed. The building trust model, The Client Trust Index™ and this book offer a way to describe trust in the business world.

When I conduct executive seminars on trust, I ask participants "What happens when customers and stakeholders trust your organization?" people talk about higher revenues, increased profits and sales, more repeat business, higher customer retention, stronger community and industry support, ease of attracting talented people, lower employee turnover rates and easier access to financial resources.

When I ask "How does it feel?" I hear: "Rewarding," "Exciting" and "Fun."

Customer and stakeholder trust affects all aspects of an organization's business. The business case is clear: companies that have the trust of their customers have a competitive advantage.

On the surface, there is widespread recognition of the importance of trust. Yet attempts to quantify trust often fall on simple measures of concept, using single statements, yes/no answers, anecdotal evidence and questions about satisfaction. I often hear executives say "We do customer satisfaction surveys," or "We have a good reputation," "We know the 'likelihood to recommend' score is good," or "We regularly ask customers for feedback." But how do you really know how much a customer trusts you, and how do you know if that actually translates into business?

For simplicity in this book, let's define customers as anyone who has the choice to accept your organization's products and services. We might really be talking about clients, students, patients, tenants, policy holders, subscribers, dealers or members. Customers may also be other departments that you work with, that use your products or services, partners, resellers or distributors. It is important to remember that all customers want what your organization promises to deliver.

Stakeholders are people who are affected by the actions of the organization.

FINDING THE CRACKS IN YOUR BUSINESS

Imagine that you're the captain of a ship far out at sea. You know the ship is taking on water, but you don't know how it's coming onboard. You plug some leaks, but you can't locate the real problem. It's coming in slowly, but you know it's only a matter of time before it becomes a crisis.

Now apply this same situation to your business. Your sales have decreased, the customers aren't as engaged as they used to be, or their contracts are coming up for renewal and they are not returning your call. You know things are not as they should be. You know you're taking on water. As the person in charge or key decision maker, you know you have to fix it.

The Client Trust Index™ exposes the cracks and the leakage. It pinpoints and triangulates where your vulnerabilities are before you sink. It can tell you how to plug the holes. It brings trust into sharper focus and provides meaningful, measureable and manageable information about your organization's and its image as a trustworthy partner in business.

The Client Trust Index™ provides factual evidence and measures true customer sentiment.

It is also a diagnostic and a survey instrument. In approximately nine minutes, a customer responds to statements about the organization's communication, behavior and service. The statements that make up the Client Trust Index™ pinpoint their trust level in the company. That produces a quantifiable score. And with that score, the organization will know on a continuum scale how they feel about a company and what the trust equity is.

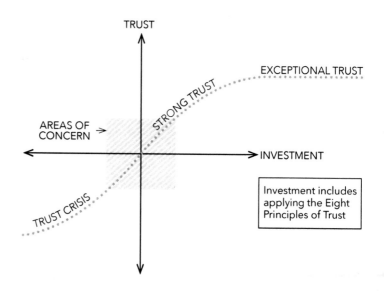

TRUST IS THE NEW CUSTOMER
KEY PERFORMANCE METRIC

The science and the evidence

In 2011, while chief marketing officer for a software company, I enrolled as a part time graduate student in a master of communications program. I focused my research on how companies build, protect, strengthen and regain trust and what drives customer behaviours. It is important to understand that I developed all of the concepts in this book by making empirical deductions directly from the data. I did not begin this project with a theory.

I started the program knowing intuitively that people look for trustworthy companies to do business with and invest in. What I actually learned, and the research I interpreted, was fascinating. I sought to build a practical model from the ground up, derived from the evidence; a methodology and a disciplined approach for organizations to apply to get results. I finished my program with a solid business case.

Based on that research, I developed a model and tool kit to help organizations build, strengthen and protect the trust their customers have in them. These techniques help build a culture of trust that acts in the customer's best interest.

Throughout my graduate studies, I researched how organizations build trust with their external stakeholders and how organizations measure it. I performed qualitative in-depth interviews with executives across Canada and the U.S. in publically recognized successful companies to determine how their organizations generate trust with their external stakeholders.

I read articles, case studies and books about trust, systematically coding the academic and business research. I wrote dozens of essays and papers, performed analyses, presented and debated and asked questions. I examined trust from many angles. Before we dive in to the model, it is important to recognize that trust means different things to different people based on their personal experiences and based on their experience, it takes some people longer to trust than others.

When customers are confident they can rely on an organization to do the right thing for them, organizational trust exists. To trust another person or organization means we have confidence in their words or actions; there is an expectation the person or organization will be reliable and act in your best interest.

Generating trust is multidimensional and according to many scholars, including Bernard Barber, author of The Logics and Limits of Trust; Niklas Luhmann, author of Trust and Power; and J. David Lewis and Andrew Weigert, authors of Trust as a Social Reality, there are three dimensions of trust: emotional, behavioural and cognitive. These three dimensions merge into an overarching social experience. The dimensions support each other and are necessary for trust to develop. Depending on the situation, one may become more dominant than the others. The behavioural dimension of trust weaves throughout the cognitive and emotional dimensions, accounting for how a person behaves in different situations.

The Social Experience

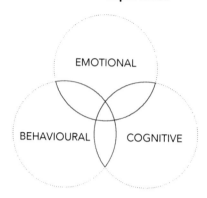

We consider the following dimensions when we are deciding to trust:

- Reliability
- Delivery
- Transparency
- Honesty
- Consistency
- Benevolent Behaviour
- Compassion
- Responsibility
- Empathy
- Vulnerability
- Risk
- Collaboration
- Mutual Understanding

- Proactive communication
- Clarity
- Dialogue
- Sharing
- Listening
- Obligation
- Obtaining feedback
- Reciprocity
- Respect
- Motivations
- Commitment
- Ethical behaviour
- Integrity

THE TRUST BUILDING MODEL

The Trust Building Model was created with the customer at the centre. At its core, the Building, Strengthening and Protecting Trust Model begins with creating a customer centered trust culture.

Peter Drucker, management consultant, educator and author says, "Culture trumps strategy every time." As discussed in the first chapter, once a culture of trust is in place with the leadership team, the next job is aligning employees with the company's purpose, mission and values.

VALUES AND CONDUCT

As Ian Cavanagh, retired partner of EY Canada, and co-founder and former CEO of Ambir says, "Culture and a company's credo is everything. Having a culture based on values and trust is the essence of any successful trustworthy organization. Culture is the secret sauce — the ingredient that goes through the entire organization."

Successful organizations have organizational values, ethics or a code of conduct, which can also be referred to as guiding principles, values credo, leadership values, the "company way," or "how to serve customers." Top companies publish, distribute and discuss codes of conduct with their employees.

When I spoke to Scott McCain, former COO of Maple Leaf Foods, about how important the company values were to Maple Leaf Foods and how they affect company decisions, he paused, got out of his chair and withdrew a laminated sheet from his briefcase. He handed it to me. "These are our values," he said. "I keep them in my briefcase; they go everywhere with me. We make all of our decisions, large and small, based on the company values."

At Bell Canada, the company's code of conduct is discussed regularly and employees sign the code of conduct annually. It can be found on the Bell corporate website in the Governance section. "At Bell Canada, we are constantly investing in our people, in our processes and in our technology so that our customers have a better experience with us," said Heather Tulk, former senior vice president at Bell Canada. "We spend a lot of time measuring, developing and improving internal relationships so our employees feel like they are operating within a system of trust, which will then put them in a position to create trust externally. This wasn't set out as a strategy to generate trust, however it contributes to creating trust."

As we discussed, building trust starts at the top with the CEO and the leadership team. When leaders value trust and communicate it across the enterprise, trust-building gets embedded and a culture of trust permeates the company. Culture affects every level of an organization and ultimately every customer through customer touch points, including sales, marketing, invoicing and delivery of services.

CAPABILITIES AND COMPETENCIES

In addition to values, and codes of conduct and ethics, organizations must possess and demonstrate capabilities and competencies. As we know, customers buy from and support organizations based on what they promise to deliver. If a company promises high quality engineering advice, for example, then the company must have the professional engineers and skilled advisors on the team to provide the advice. Capabilities are table stakes, a must have; and capabilities are tangible elements of trust.

Organizations can demonstrate and show capabilities through:
- Qualifications and skills of employees including education level and professional designations
- Experience including number of years, and types of projects
- Licenses
- Certifications
- References of customers or industry thought leaders
- Customer testimonials and case studies
- Photographs of projects completed with customers

- Systems and processes
- Proper equipment and facilities
- Qualified staff
- Third-party recognition of awards
- Stating the number of years the organization has been in business
- Listing the customers it has worked with
- Publishing white papers, reports and research
- Adhering to industry standards

COMMUNICATION, BEHAVIOUR AND SERVICE

When these foundational elements are in place, specific methods of communicating, behaving and serving contribute to building, strengthening and protecting trust.

These underlying elements are present and offer support when customers are deciding to trust. The emotional, cognitive and behavioural science is built into this model. The Eight Principles of Building, Strengthening and Protecting Trust were developed from the underlying elements, decision criteria and dimensions of trust.

THE EIGHT PRINCIPLES OF BUILDING, PROTECTING AND STRENGTHENING TRUST

1. Listen carefully with empathy and compassion, question and involve the customer or stakeholder in a dialogue

2. Communicate using clear, concrete and conversational language

3. Be honest and transparent

4. Be consistent, predictable and reliable

5. Act in the best interests of customers, stakeholders and the public

6. Do the right thing. If you make a mistake, fix it

7. Deliver on your promise

8. Commit to the long term

Trust has energy. It can grow and develop. It is time based.
Trust is assessed and reassessed continually over time through
experiences with the organization and its critical trust risk points.
Critical trust risk points are experiences people have with an
organization's leaders, experts and employees as well as with their
products, services, offerings and communications.

Trust Building Model

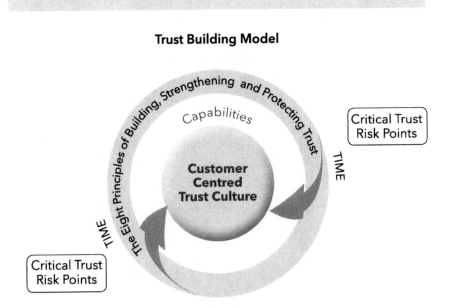

This Building Trust Model has been presented at academic conferences, has
appeared in conference proceedings of the world's largest academic conference for
communication scholars, the International Communication Association conference in San Juan, Puerto Rico, and has appeared in a "poster session."

At the time this book was being completed, the model had been accepted for
publication in the Canadian Journal of Communication, a peer-reviewed academic
journal. Peer review is a process used by publishers and editors of academic and

scholarly journals to ensure the articles they publish meet the accepted standards of their discipline. Peer reviewers evaluate the quality of the scholarship, reliability of the findings, and the research and relevance to the field of study.

MEASURING TRUST

As previously mentioned, Peter Drucker tells us that what can be managed can be measured, and with this in mind I created the Client Trust Index™. I have always believed that organizations should start with data, facts and research. So I investigated how companies can measure their customer's trust in them.

A few models and measures to evaluate organizational trust have been created over the years, including Anthony Athos and John Gabarro's trust in employer; Larry Cummings and Philip Bromiley's organizational trust inventory; Hurley's decision to trust model to assess levels of trust within organizations; and Pamela Shockley- Zalabak et al.'s model to measure trust within organizations. These models measure trust inside an organization. However there have only been limited attempts to measure an external customer's or stakeholder's trust in an organization.

My desire to better understand how trust is measured among an organization's customers and external stakeholders inspired me to develop the Client Trust Index™. This assessment tool incorporates the scientific dimensions of trust, along with behaviours and criteria that individuals use to determine if they trust an organization and their level of trust.

In our digital economy, with its multitude of choices, trust is more important than ever before. We know that if people trust you, they'll buy your products and services. If they don't trust you, they tell everyone they know. As you will see, I have dedicated a tremendous amount of time and resources to researching best practices of how consumers, customers and stakeholders decide to trust and how organizations go about building and protecting trust.

> The Trust Building Model is a framework for organizations to follow to build, strengthen and protect trust with customers.

TESTING THE CLIENT TRUST INDEX™

The Client Trust Index™ went through the same phases as any empirically tested measurement tool. It started as part of my master's research, which aimed to create a measurement tool so companies could understand how well they were trusted by customers and stakeholders.

The first test of the Client Trust Index™ was a pre-test. This was completed within academia. Next, it was tested on commercial businesses. I used three different types of companies of different sizes and industries: an ICT firm, a manufacturing company and a global company that trades on the NYSE. To complete the advanced empirical testing and to demonstrate it as a valid measurement of trust, I needed to measure it against multiple variables. I also needed a larger sample.

I contacted a national Canadian organization and it agreed to take part. The organization, which provides products and services across Canada, has a variety of national customers, some new, some that have been customers for more than 35 years. I brought in an expert in data analytics and research methods and conducted the Client Trust Index™ on a sample of the firm's customers.

I worked with Dr. Alla Kushrink, assistant professor at Mount Saint Vincent University; Dr. Binod Sundararajan, associate director of Rowe School of Business, Dalhousie University; and Alyssa Simon, a graduate student at Mount Saint Vincent University.

This research project broadened the scope of the testing to increase the sample and population size. An electronic survey was sent to 19,500 customers. Survey responses to each item were measured on a seven-point Likert scale ranging from

"Strongly Agree" (seven) to "Strongly Disagree" (one), with verbal labels for scale points two through six.

Higher scores represented higher, more positive attitudes of trust toward the organization. Our main goal with this data collection was to evaluate robustness of the instrument. We wanted to test the validity of the tool against recognized standards and prove that The Eight Principles of Building, Strengthening and Protecting Trust are in fact how customers and stakeholders decide whether or not to trust an organization.

In addition to testing the validity and reliability of the Client Trust Index™ and the Eight Principles of Trust as the decision criteria individuals use to trust an organization, we proposed and tested six hypotheses:

H1: There is a positive relationship between trust and relationship satisfaction with an organization.

H2: There is a positive relationship between trust and overall satisfaction with an organization.

H3: There is a positive relationship between trust and the likelihood to recommend an organization.

H4: There is a positive relationship between trust and loyalty to an organization.

H5: There is a positive relationship between trust and commitment to an organization.

H6: There is a positive relationship between trust and a customer's intent to continue using an organization's products and services.

This primary research and the final phase in the development of the Client Trust Index™ confirmed the statistically significant correlation between trust and customer commitment, loyalty, satisfaction, likelihood to recommend, and continuation of buying products and services.

The Client Trust Index™ was tested over four years through four phases of the development of empirically tested assessment tool. An overview of these phases is outlined in Table 1.

PHASES OF DEVELOPMENT TESTING

Phase	Activity	Time Line
Phase 1: Qualitative in-depth interviews with executives	Initial sample size 10; which led to the creation and development of the Principles of Trust. Input was included from academic literature. Participants' responses support content validity	Six months
Phase 2: Scale item creation	Based on Eight Principles of Building, Strengthening and Protecting Trust from phase 1; participants' responses and literature were used to generate scale items. Items generated with input from the expert panel review supports content validity. The scale was tested with university students in a closed environment.	Six months
Phase 3: Scale Refinement	Evaluation and refinement of items and survey instrument and directions. Tested with several companies in several industries with a population size of approximately 800. Companies included Fortune 500 companies traded on the NYSE.	Two years
Phase 4: Construct and Criteria Validity Testing	Testing and analysis of Client Trust Index™ with Canadian organization with 80,000 customers and a sample size of 19,500. Testing in this phase included psychometric analysis; internal reliability testing. Alpha's levels were excellent. We used exploratory factor analysis to test the construct's validity. All items loaded strongly on three factors; and confirmatory factor analysis for criterion validity.	One year

I set out to quantify trust. I can now objectively demonstrate the correlation between trust and profit. That means organizations can benchmark it, develop strategies to address trust gaps and measure again. We have done this for companies and they have been rewarded with positive results. Customers tell me how powerful it is. We can chart progress and design programs around it because it is quantifiable and directly relates to short and long-term profits.

When it was all said and done, the total project consumed approximately seven person years of effort. We read and systematically coded hundreds of articles, generated dozens of pages of interview transcripts and sheets and sheets of raw data. Each phase along the way was built upon the one before it until we were able to see and understand the critical role of trust and how we make the profound decision to trust or not to trust.

THREE CASES

Here are three cases taken from my own consulting practice in which the Client Trust Index™ was used in practical business situations. In the interests of client confidentiality I am not naming the companies involved.

ORGANIZATION A is a Canadian multinational manufacturing company that sells multiple product lines in 20 countries. Its customers are industry specific and include medium and large Fortune 1000 organizations. The company experienced a year of significant change on a number of fronts, including new account managers, new products and new distributors. Sales were decreasing, long-term customers were buying less and its representatives were not being invited to strategic meetings with their customers. The company did not feel as close to its customers as it had in the past but couldn't pinpoint why. Top managers didn't know where or what the problem was.

The company was planning to refresh its brand and launch new products and services. It wanted a strategy based on evidence, facts and customer insights. The Client Trust Index™ report and the results revealed hidden vulnerabilities and specific behavioural changes necessary to stop the erosion in sales. Its overall trust equity was lower than they anticipated. After reviewing the Client Trust Index™ results, the organization developed and implemented trust strengthening and protecting actions and decisions. Within one year of completing the Client Trust Index™, and implementing the recommended actions for improvement, the company reported an increase in profits, sales revenue and customer engagement.

Organization A

Deliver on your promise

Listen carefully, with empathy and compassion, question and involve

Communicate using clear, concrete conversational language

Be consistent, predictable and reliable

Be honest and transparent

Do the right thing. If you make a mistake, fix it.

Commit to the long term

Act in the best interest of customers

ORGANIZATION B is an international S&P 500 company, publicly traded on the NYSE, headquartered in the U.S. The company provides services to a specific sector. The landscape in North America has changed economically, socially and politically in the last 20 years. There have been regulatory changes and new entrants in the market. The changing dynamics, coupled with the company's goal of excellence in stakeholder relations and continuous improvement made it timely for them to evaluate stakeholder sentiment and create a benchmark. Organizational stakeholders surveyed included community and business leaders, educational institutions, members of government as well as environmental and conservation stakeholders.

Findings and insights from The Client Trust Index™ identified where Organization B was doing well, areas for improvement and insights that contributed in developing organizational strategy. After analyzing the data, trust strengthening and protective actions and decisions were recommended. Within six months of completing the Client Trust Index™, stakeholders were found to be more engaged with Organization B, as measured by the number of inbound calls of inquiry to the organization, the number of requests to speak at conferences and the number of requests to participate in industry discussions.

Twelve months after the initial benchmark was established, Organization B measured its trust equity conducting the Client Trust Index™ again. The trust equity improved with stakeholders and market segments in which it focused and its Client Trust Index™ score increased slightly overall.

Organization B

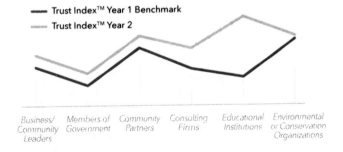

— Trust Index™ Year 1 Benchmark
— Trust Index™ Year 2

Business/   Members of   Community   Consulting   Educational   Environmental
Community   Government   Partners   Firms   Institutions   or Conservation
Leaders   Organizations

ORGANIZATION C is an Information and Communications Technology (ICT) company. The company markets and supports it's professional services, and resells technology products regionally. The company is well known for providing excellent customer service and innovative products. In fact, offering a superior customer experience is central to its brand. Customer referrals have filled the sales funnel for many years.

Organization C experienced early indicators of decreased customer trust and customer commitment. Specifically, there was a decrease in the number of customer referrals, the number of customer support issues were increasing, and sales were declining. Coupled with these signals, Organization C had made changes to its customer support processes and personnel. A few customers mentioned the changes.

The senior management in the organization knew they needed to make adjustments to the customer experience. They wanted to improve the customer experience, address the issues and increase sales. Senior management needed to know what specific behaviours and actions were required to improve performance.

After analyzing the data, trust strengthening actions were developed for Organization C.

Within three months, sales increased, the number of referrals started to rise, and customer support issues decreased by 70 per cent.

Organization C

Be consistent, predictable and reliable

Be honest and transparent

Deliver on your promise

Communicate using clear, concrete conversational language

Act in the best interests of customers

Commit to the long term

Do the right thing. If you make a mistake, fix it.

Listen carefully, with empathy and compassion, question and involve

The Client Trust Index™ had its origins in academia but it is rooted in the real world. The scientific method was applied to identify the patterns, causes and effects of creating trust within the business world.

The Science and the Evidence Confirms:
- Trust can be measured; it is quantifiable.
- The Eight Principles of Trust are in fact how customers and stakeholders decide to trust an organization.
- When an organization or individual applies the Eight Principles of Trust to how it communicates, behaves and serves customers, trust will be built, strengthened, and protected.
- An organization's Client Trust Index™ score is a predictor of future success; specifically the customer's likelihood to continue to buy its products and services and its likelihood to recommend the company, its products and/or its services.
- The Client Trust Index™ score is a measurement and predictor of loyalty and commitment.
- Trust affects the bottom line.

3

First Impressions:
We Trust What We Believe,
See and Experience

It has been said that how we look and the tone of our body language speak so loudly that people sometimes can't hear what we are saying with our words. We instinctively trust what we see before we trust what we hear.

First impressions are made within a few seconds. When we meet someone, we form an opinion of them right away. The next four minutes are spent validating that impression. If the first impression isn't right, it usually takes a full seven minutes to change it.

Customers judge us on the little things, so be aware of the first impression you leave and the message you are sending. You are a representative of your company. Are you and your company represented in a good light if you show up late for a meeting wearing a wrinkled suit and ask to borrow a pen? Customers want to be impressed. They want a meeting with you to be a good use of their time. They want to build trust with you right away.

The way you present yourself makes a huge difference in how you are perceived and how you are regarded. We subconsciously evaluate the following when we meet someone:

+ Facial expressions
+ Clothes and grooming

- Posture and mannerisms
- Gestures
- Listening
- Handshake
- Language

TRUST AND BODY LANGUAGE

Trust is at the heart of every interaction. First we decide if we trust, then we decide about an organization's capabilities.

Body language experts are also discovering this. Dr. Amy Cuddy, a psychologist at Harvard University, has been studying body language for 10 years. She and her colleagues have found that when you make instant judgments about other people we're answering two primary questions: Can I trust this person? And, can I trust this person's capabilities? According to Cuddy's research, 80 to 90 per cent of a first impression is based on trust and capability.

Cuddy warns that "If someone you're trying to influence doesn't trust you, you aren't going to get very far. In fact, you might even elicit suspicion, because you'll come off as manipulative."

If you don't have trust, people perceive competence as negative. The research shows this and we know this intuitively. Without trust there's a threat to the relationship. Once you recognize the significance of trustworthiness over capability, you can take control of your first impression.

Mastering body and facial Language

Body language tells a lot about someone. We can usually tell if someone is open, confident, enthusiastic or alternatively, in a bad mood. Professional speech coaches advise people to never cross their arms over their chests while speaking, and instead to use gestures and to place their hands and arms in the ready position. But there is no real right or wrong. In the mosaic of body language, there is a lot of grey area.

Experts on body language believe that we show our true feelings and our true thoughts through our body language and our movement. The body shows people how you feel and what you are thinking. People also react to body language. If you are acting fidgety and nervous, the customer is going to be sensitive to this and feel uncomfortable.

Be Authentic. Align your messages and your non-verbal communications with your natural inclinations. Know yourself and your body will follow. Do what comes naturally. The most effective gestures are spontaneous ones.

I once taught a course on presentation skills and one of the students did her speech on how to make the perfect chocolate chip cookie. She held a fictitious bowl in the middle of her talk and stirred that batter like a pro. She had us so involved in the talk that we all wanted cookies. If you try to incorporate rules and tips that don't seem natural to you, you risk looking like a robot. Do what comes naturally to produce the most effective gestures.

A smile goes a long way

> *"A man without a smiling face must not open a shop."*
> - Ancient Chinese Proverb

A sincere smile is the simplest first step to a good first impression. It doesn't matter if your teeth are crooked, straight, bleached or coffee stained. Your smile costs nothing, but it has the effect of creating a positive first impression. Your smile is a message of your goodwill.

The effect of a smile is powerful, even when it isn't seen. When you smile while talking on the phone, your smile comes through in your voice. If you smile at people, you will get noticed. You will find that people smile back at you. When you smile, it warms the room. It makes people feel more comfortable.

Think about it. If you start a conversation with a frown, how will the person respond to you? They'll wonder what's troubling you. Are you upset? Are you angry? They'll be ill at ease. When you start your conversation or a presentation with a sincere smile, your audience will respond in kind. They'll relax and listen. A smile sets the mood of a conversation. If you smile it will help lift your own spirits. It will help your own mindset. What you put out to people you will receive back.

Smiling generates more orders to sales reps, more tips to those in the service industry, and creates a friendlier atmosphere in most work environments.

A few years ago, I was asked to do a Ted X Talk on trust. I was excited, honoured and nervous. I was anxious because all Ted X Talks are recorded live and can be found online. After 20 years in the IT industry, I know that online means permanent. But I knew it was the right thing to do, since my new company was just getting off the ground. So I did all the things I would advise a customer to do: I wrote my speech, carefully thought about what I was going to wear, checked the venue and logistics and practiced my presentation. I practiced and practiced and practiced, sometimes walking around the house rehearsing my talk. Typically I do not practice in front of people. However, this time, my daughter who was 10 at the time, was watching.

"Are you presenting to mean people?" she asked me. "Do you not like those people?" I said, "Why would you say that?" She said I looked unhappy. What I learned in that moment was that I'm not a natural smiler. I always thought I was, but as it turned out, I wasn't. Now I make a conscious effort to smile, I think about it. Smiling is something we can control.

Several years ago I gave a presentation to about 200 European technology professions at an event in Malaga, Spain. A professional comedian introduced me at a live question and answer session. I didn't know many people in the audience. It was an important event, as everyone listening was a potential customer and I had to do a good job for my company.

I looked at the audience, as many do in this situation, for support.

One particular man smiled at me through the entire presentation. His smile was sincere, warm and authentic. It made me feel more comfortable, which was the most important part. I went to speak to him after and learned he was Italian and spoke many languages, however, he spoke very little English. He had a translator with him throughout the conference.

As far as first impressions go, I had a good impression of him because of his genuine and authentic smile. His facial expression demonstrated interest in my presentation. With a smile, it's more than how we move our mouth and lips. Our eyes show our sincerity. It didn't even matter that he couldn't speak English; I just connected with him.

The presentation worked out very well in the end, and our company won some new business, including from the Italian man in the audience who spoke very little English.

People can tell if you are giving them a sincere smile. Amateur photographers will ask their subjects to say cheese, good photographers get the subject to laugh and brilliant photographers snap you in the act.

When presenting at seminars, I will often show a 60-second video clip without any sound. It's a video of a person talking and interacting with other people. The video shows a businesswoman doing a presentation and then going into a Q&A around a table with other business people.

After the video, I ask the seminar participants to tell me about this person. What I'm really asking is, what does her body language tell us? What does it tell us about the way she communicates? Nine times out of 10, the seminar participants describe her to a tee. I know this because the video is of someone I know and do business with. But it doesn't matter if I know them or not, because a person's body language is what he or she is communicating.

I ask their opinion on the following descriptive words, as they relate to the subject in the video:

- Uptight
- Approachable
- Darting eyes
- Pleasant
- Relaxed
- Good listener
- Impatient
- Friendly
- Clean cut
- Flashy
- Substance
- Professional
- Listener

- Patient
- Smile
- Frown
- Bored
- Unprepared
- Disrespectful
- Fidgeting
- Sighing
- On edge
- Calm
- High-level executive
- Clothes
- Friends

What is amazing to me, is regardless of whether I play the video for 10 seconds or 60 seconds, those who watch it usually say the same things. About 90 per cent of the participants' responses and observations are bang on.

This applies to all areas of life and work. At work, if we come out of a meeting wearing a scowl, are annoyed or visibly upset, our colleagues are going to suspect it didn't go well. They'll know from the body language whether it was a good meeting or a bad one. When my husband comes home from work I can tell just by the way he acts if he had a good or bad day. Customers can tell too.

Even if we don't know the other person that well, a person's body language communicates a message. I often ask seminar participants to consider the body language of the people around them. What does it say about them?

THE RIGHT KIND OF IMPRESSION

The following are examples of three trusted people who left the wrong kind of impression because of their body language.

Soprano Bill: Six years ago I was in Long Island, New York to meet a customer for the first time. I had a relationship with this person by email and phone only, and had no real opinion of him. I had no idea how old he was or what he looked like. All I knew was that he was the decision maker as to whether they would be a distributor of our product, or not.

My colleague and I were introduced to the man, who we will call Bill for the purpose of this anecdote. Bill was six-foot-three, heavy set, had gelled jet-black hair, dressed in head-to-toe black, and had a stern look on his face. His size commanded the boardroom. He shook my hand so firmly it hurt. He then began to speak in a thick New York accent. He talked slowly and was still barely audible. He didn't gesture and he didn't move.

After leaving the office, I asked my colleague what he thought of Bill. He replied, "Sopranos," he said, referring to the popular television series about life in the Mafia. "Clearly 'Bill' is the boss. I wouldn't mess with him."

We didn't know what Bill's intentions were. We didn't think he was going to do what he said he was going to do. And although he signed a contract with us, we didn't believe he would follow through on his promise.

Our conclusion on this first impression: Not trustworthy. We didn't think he was going to do what he said he was going to do. We were suspicious of him, we felt like he was hiding something.

Dead Eyes Tim: A few years ago I attended a conference and trade show in Washington, DC. I travelled with a colleague who was relatively new to the industry. I introduced her around and we headed to visit our partners' booth, which was staffed by one of our associates. As we were walking through the aisles she pointed to a man in a booth and said to me, "Look at that guy, he has dead eyes." And she was right. He didn't look approachable; he appeared bored, uninterested and uncomfortable. It looked like he didn't want to be there. She added, "I hope that's not the guy you want me to meet."

Unfortunately, it was. I knew him and I knew he was excited about the conference. He was moderating the panel and this conference was a big deal for his company and ours. We were launching a new product to the cable industry. He was also our most senior executive at the conference. The booth looked fabulous, with one of the nicest displays on the entire trade show floor. However, the person manning the booth had "dead eyes" and was totally unapproachable to others.

It doesn't matter if we just caught him deep in thought or having just hung up from a bad phone call. When you're standing at a booth at a conference, the first impression you're giving off—your visual—has to be a good one.

Our conclusion on this first impression: Unapproachable and not trustworthy.

Intense and Hyper Ingrid: One of my customers is an experienced pharmaceutical sales representative. Let's call her Ingrid. During one of our coaching sessions Ingrid was telling me about how disappointed she was about a referral she didn't get. I asked her to describe the meeting to me. She said she drove three hours to get to her appointment, which was with a new specialist in her region. I asked her to describe the meeting.

It was 9 a.m. and she was full of excitement, anxious to explain a new study that demonstrated how her product would be beneficial to this doctor's patients. While describing the meeting she realized she spoke very fast, shook hands firmly, but too quickly. It was difficult for her to contain herself, and she recalled describing the study while taking off her coat. She said she had a lot of energy, as if she'd just had a double shot of espresso.

I asked her: What kinds of questions and comments did the specialist have about the new study? Her answer: None

It sounded as if the doctor could not get a word in edgewise. The sales representative did not stop talking or moving for 10 minutes, which was the entire length of the visit.

When presenting new study results loaded with detailed information, a slower pace of speech with smaller or more controlled movements and fewer gestures may have made a stronger impact. People subconsciously associate confidence with calm, controlled body style, purposeful body movements and talking in a slower pace. It's crucial that we listen, empathize and pay close attention to the customer's priorities. As I say to some of my clients, when you're telling, you're not selling.

Our conclusion on hearing this account of this first impression: poor listener with lack of empathy.

COMMUNICATING TRUST IN THE WORKPLACE

Your workplace should put forward the same type of positive first impression that you do. Here are a few "not so obvious" things that communicate trust or distrust in a company.

1. Location of office
Consider the physical appearance of your business. Where is the building? What is the neighbourhood like? What is the space like outside the building? Are the gardens and grass well kept?

The corporate head office building of the Four Seasons Hotels and Resorts, in Toronto, has the same high-end luxury feel as one of their hotels. When you step inside the lobby, it is as beautiful as any lobby in one of their hotels. There are paintings on the wall, a portrait of the founder, high quality furnishings, brochures and hardcover books that display Four Seasons' properties around the world.

When you walk through the halls on the main floor there is a map of the world with pinpoints of where their hotels are.

2. Inside décor

Inside, look at the wall colours. Are they appropriate? What is the quality of the furnishings? Is it clean and tidy? Are the lights on? Is it too bright? Is it too dark? Consider the sounds. Is soothing music playing? Are the sounds of a busy office distracting? Are phones ringing? Or is there too much silence? Is the signage nicely displayed and does it match the brand?

Visitors and customers will often spend a fair amount of time in your waiting room. If the company has received awards and or been recognized in the industry, displaying the certificates, plaques in the lobby can communicate accomplishments to employees and guests. Consider the available reading material. Is it appropriate? If you have a message on a digital screen or physical sign, does it support the organization's branding? The waiting room provides an opportunity to make a first impression.

A company that does business in the entertainment industry may have People Magazine, newspapers and entertainment publications, where an architectural firm may consider having design magazines and newspapers.

Many companies use their waiting areas to promote their brands and their ideas. The Shaw Group in Halifax, Nova Scotia and McCain Foods in Florenceville, New Brunswick and Cox and Palmer in Saint John, New Brunswick for example, display books about the history of their companies. Wilson Fuels in Halifax, Nova Scotia displays historical company photographs on the walls. At the Cox Communications office in Las Vegas, Nevada their vision and mission is displayed on the wall. At the CNN headquarters in Atlanta, the network's programming is carried non-stop on wall-mounted screens. Other companies display their values, code of conduct or ethics and awards in their front lobby areas.

When a company displays signage, awards and/or reading material, it is not only communicating the corporate identity, they are empowering guests with information, therefore acting in the guest's best interests, while building credibility and familiarity at the same time.

3. Office greeting

Upon arrival, who is the first person your customers or guests' meet? Are guests greeted with an immediate smile? Guests should always be made to feel comfortable. One way to do this is to offer a cup of coffee or tea or a glass of water, and offer to take the person's coat.

Respect for the other person's time is paramount in the business world. None of us want to be kept waiting more than a few minutes. Any longer than that, and we start to wonder what is more important than my visit?

I have visited countless offices over the years and many stand out in my memory as welcoming. One such time was when I visited the Commissionaires' Canada office. The organization's motto is "Trusted – Everyday - Everywhere." When I arrived, the commissionaire at the front desk acknowledged my meeting with a smile and said the person I was meeting "is expecting you. This is your security pass. He will be right out."

Being welcoming and prepared gives the impression that you and your company are organized and dependable. Both are characteristics that build trust.

4. Uniforms

Uniforms are more relevant today than ever before because they're a practical way for a company to build and protect trust.

Uniforms can:

1. Communicate professionalism
2. Reinforce a brand
3. Promote consistency by managing what employees are wearing
4. Foster familiarity

Uniforms efficiently and quickly communicate that the person is an employee with a particular company. Uniforms can strengthen brands. They indicate that the company is concerned about its employees' appearance. A uniform can be a blazer, a shirt, or a sweater that uses the corporate colour scheme.

Seeing a uniform we've seen before promotes a sense of familiarity and unconsciously affects how we trust. For example, even if we do not know the package delivery driver, when we see the UPS brown, it communicates UPS and we trust that brand. UPS has actually copyrighted the colour brown that they use in their uniforms and in their logo. The UPS uniforms communicate consistency, predictability and reliability, which is Principle #4 of building and protecting customer trust.

If your business doesn't require a uniform, and many don't, implementing a dress code can help achieve the same results. Regardless, you should always dress in professional, clean, well-tailored clothing. Make sure your clothing is neatly ironed and free of pet hair. Lab coats for doctors, pharmacists, scientists and dentists project professionalism and tell us what a person does, which reinforces a brand.

First we decide if we trust, then we decide
about an organization's capabilities.

~

Trust is at the heart of every interaction.

4

Becoming a Trusted Advisor

Everybody needs advice from time to time, in our personal and family lives and in our work. Often, good advice makes the difference between success and disaster. When we need that vital guidance, we seek out a professional we can trust: a trusted advisor.

Websites, magazines, blogs and books can offer information and sometimes insight, but cannot provide the personalized services of a trusted advisor. Customers want to share their ideas, plans and concerns with someone who understands them. They want to work with people who are smart, trusted and focused on their interests. Trust is not something you can buy in today's complex, mediated society. Professionals have to earn it, and work to keep it.

We've seen how earning the trust of your customers, partners, suppliers and prospects is critical to your long-term success as a professional. According to the 2011 Edelman Trust Barometer, 80 per cent of people buy from people they trust, while 68 per cent recommend a person they trust to a friend or colleague. Whether your goal is to sustain sales growth or improve the experience your customers have with your organization, having your customers' trust is imperative.

EVERYTHING STARTS WITH THE CUSTOMER

Every customer wants to feel important. Some want to believe their interests are the most important in the world. A trusted advisor will get to know their customers and their customers' needs. They will be there to offer independent, relevant advice to the people they are doing business with. They are not trying to sell to their customers. They are compassionate about their customer's situation. They want to help.

I have a travel agent I trust. She is my trusted advisor when it comes to travel. When I travel for business she knows my needs, preferences and expectations. For example, she knows to put me on the most direct route, and that I like an aisle seat. I don't mind flying out at 6 a.m. and I don't mind getting home at midnight. When she arranges travel for my family, it is a different situation. She knows my family is not good with 6 a.m. or midnight flights. She would never suggest a vacation spot just to sell a vacation package, and she would never advocate for a trip that is not in my family's best interest. For example, she wouldn't put us on a cruise where passengers can't get off the boat or there isn't entertainment for my children. She knows we want to go somewhere that we can see and experience the local culture. She knows my priorities, expectations, plans and budget. If she doesn't know something, she asks the right kinds of questions to add value and to make recommendations. Sometimes she suggests we use a discounted travel site to get a better rate. She is a trusted advisor because she acts in our best interests.

When you and your employees become trusted advisors both the company and your customers reap the benefits.

Trusted Advisors:

- Put customer interests first
- Communicate in a conversational tone
- Speak the language of trust, by building trust verbally and with their body language.
- Listen actively and with empathy
- Are compassionate
- Abide by a code of conduct
- Commit to relationships for the long term
- Make sure employees are fully informed and versed in their area of expertise
- Identify customer concerns
- Provide services without necessarily being compensated
- Are straightforward and candid with their advice
- Anticipate customer needs
- Strive to understand what the customer is really asking
- Make informed suggestions
- Describe issues on the customer's terms
- Can adapt their communication and behaviour styles with customers
- Recommend a competitor's solution if it is better for the customer
- Set and manage expectations
- Build long-term trusting relationships

Trusted advisors are empowered to serve customers. They are informed and educated. They get the solutions right and solve customer problems and issues.

Trusted advisors impress, wow and amaze customers in how they serve, they act in the customer's best interests and are motivated to help. Typically they are master communicators. They are great listeners, so they are able to identify customer concerns and determine the value they can provide. As one of our seminar participants said, "trusted advisors understand their customers, they get them."

Trusted advisors apply the eight principles to building trust to their behaviour in the work place and with customers. Any company or organization that wants to build trust with its customers and stakeholders must encourage all employees to become trusted advisors to customers.

TRUSTED ADVISORS PUT THEMSELVES IN THEIR CUSTOMERS' SHOES

"Why are they asking for this? Why don't they just download the file? I wish they would just decide what they want and stop making so many changes. Why can't they make a decision? Why are they calling over the lunch hour? That is not our policy, I have told them so many times. Why are they are always distracted? Why are we always waiting for them? Why are they are so slow? If the customer would just follow our purchasing process then everything would be fine."

Do you ever hear people in your company asking these questions or making statements like these about your customers? If you do, these are clear indicators that the company may not actually be acting in the customer's best interest, that your organization may not be as focused on the customer as it could be or that you do not know enough about the customer and their situation.

All customers are looking for professionals they can trust. More specifically, they are looking for trusted advisors. Customers want to buy from and work with people and organizations that focus on them, with people who understand their situation, and ultimately with people they can trust. Computers, websites, books and how-to guides can't provide this. It is about people.

Every customer wants to feel special. They want to feel that that are a very important customer to you and your organization. Customers expect the front line customer service employees and personnel to be knowledgeable and helpful on just about any question they have.

When we understand the customer's situation we can anticipate their questions and concerns. Understanding and anticipating is key to acting in the customer's best interests.

The following are questions and concerns customers often have on their minds:

1. "Will this person be friendly and will they be patient with me?"
2. "Will I be pressured? I do not want to be pressured into making decisions."
3. "Will they explain themselves clearly and in terms I understand?"
4. "Will they be sympathetic to my lack of knowledge and personal concerns?"
5. "Will they make an effort to fully understand my situation?"
6. "Will I be embarrassed when I reveal my situation?"
7. "Will they try to sell me products or services I do not need or want?"
8. "Are they going to fully disclose the costs and the fees if I act on the recommendations they make?"
9. "Will they give me ample notification if there are changes to my fees or other policies?"
10. "Can I be completely frank with them about my situation?"
11. "Are they going to address all of my concerns?"

12. "It would be great if they would just look after this for me without any hassle."
13. "Will they protect my personal and confidential information?"
14. "Will they keep our discussions in confidence?"
15. "Will they be respectful and polite with my colleagues?"
16. "Will they do what they say they are going to do?"
17. "Will they act in my best interests?"
18. "If I encounter a problem, will they fix it?"
19. "Are they going to be difficult to work with?"
20. "Do I like them?"
21. "Will they see the project through?"

Holistically understanding your customer's situation is an important step to building, strengthening or protecting trust with them. Medical doctors are often very skilled at this. They are trained to diagnose, to find out what's really wrong and suggest ways to fix it. Think about the last time you met with a doctor for a routine check up. You sit in the office and your doctor has a file open about you and your health. The doctor asks a number of open-ended questions to get a sense of how you are doing: "*What brings you here today, or what is going on? How is everything going with you? Any issues or concerns you want to talk about today? Any changes since we met last? Is anything bothering you? Now tell me about that, How long has this been going on?*"

Do you know your customer's situation? When we know, we can help them solve their issues or offer them support. When we look the customer from the customer's point of view, we put ourselves in their shoes and we become more effective trusted advisors.

The answers to the following questions about your customers will bring you closer to understanding their situation:

- What worries them and what doesn't?
- What kind of job or career do they have?
- Is their position secure?
- Are they well informed?
- Is the organization where they work stable?
- What is the environment like? Stressful or pleasant?
- Do they have privacy at work or are they in an open environment?
- What is their personal life like?
- What is the state of health?
- Family situation?
- Personal Interests?
- What do they do in their spare time?
- Education level?
- Who and what influence them?
- How do they make decisions?
- Are they short-term thinkers or long-term thinkers?
- What is their money philosophy?
- What motivates them?

Motivation can be tricky to figure out. There is often an emotional dimension to a customer's motivation. In many cases, it is personal. Regardless of how tricky or personal it is, finding out what motivates your customer is an important piece to the overall holistic picture of your customer.

Keeping in mind that everyone is unique, understand that your customer is a person. Your customer and his or her company may be motivated by very different things than you are.

Consider the following potential motivations:

- the prospect of a promotion
- to be first
- to win
- to seek support for a decision already made or being considered
- fear of failure or not doing a good job
- recognition of a job or project well done
- achieving a milestone or making a deadline
- looking good in front of colleagues and peers in the company or in the industry
- recognition within an industry
- to win a prize, or an award or a bonus
- to be seen as a team player or to be seen as a pillar in the community

---

Others are motivated to work to go home to their family, others are motivated by pride, others by the need to excel, others to keep their job or have their contract extended. Knowing what motivates your customer can help you frame an issue and prepare for a discussion.

Customers are people too. I worked with a company several years ago on a project and when it was finished, the firm was nominated for and won an award for its project from a North American industry association. After the award ceremony, the lead executive thanked us for the project's success. He told me that he was grateful to the company and to the project because it got him a promotion with a raise. This was significant to his family because his wife had been laid off six months earlier and his extra pay would contribute to the medical bills for a sick child who was in and out of the hospital. We all knew he was married and the team knew he had children. None of us knew his wife was laid off or that he had a sick child. We did not truly know his situation.

Answering these questions and others like them bring you closer to knowing what is important to the customer. For example, some worry about their health, some like conflict and competition and some don't, some just like to talk about sports, history or politics, others have no interest in any of those things.

DEEP DIVE - WHAT IS IMPORTANT TO CUSTOMERS WHEN DEALING WITH A FINANCIAL ADVISOR?

Customers hire us to assess trustworthiness and to learn how to build strengthen or protect trust with their customers. On behalf of one my clients, I interviewed a few of their customers to get a sense of what is important to them when dealing with a financial advisor. The following is a direct quote from one of my client's customers.

"I need to talk to someone that I can get independent advice that is relevant to me. Someone who is not trying to sell me something. From someone who will not look at me as a commission cheque. I don't want the pressure to have to decide on the spot either. I don't know much about finances or money management, so it is somewhat uncomfortable and unnerving for me when I meet them because it's embarrassing, I don't really know what they are talking about most of the time."

This quote is from a customer who is the Vice President of a successful business with a net income of $145,000. He is a university educated, 45-year-old divorced man with three children. Portfolio size: $150,000.

And here is another direct quote from another customer of the same firm and the same financial advisor:

"I don't feel pressure, I may go call them about a mutual fund, or strike up a conversation to find out what I should do. I don't mind calling my advisor because I don't feel any pressure, she never tries to sell me anything. I do a bit of investing and research on my own, my degree is in finance. She just wants to help me. Odds are I will invest more with her at some point in time. I need an advisor for advise."

This quote is from a customer who is a retail clerk in a Whole Foods grocery store and a bookkeeper at night with a household net income of $68,000. She is 42 years old, university educated, married with two children. Her husband stays home with the children. Portfolio size: $250,000.

CUSTOMERS ARE PEOPLE TOO

In their book, The Millionaire Next Door, Thomas Stanley and William Danko illustrate through the stories of Doctor North and Doctor South that America's wealthiest people don't live in Beverly Hills or on Park Avenue. They live next door.

> Every customer is different and every customer's situation is unique. As the old saying goes, "you can't judge a book by its cover."

When I work with companies and conduct seminars, we take the time to think about the customer's situation holistically. We take the time to 'place ourselves in our customer's shoes.' The activity includes outlining what a customer's typical day is like, who they interact with, what their work space looks like and so on. We have done this with bankers, engineers, retailers, accountants, software and ICT companies, energy companies, funeral directors, insurers, non profit organizations who serve members and sponsors, health care providers, transportation companies, construction companies and more.

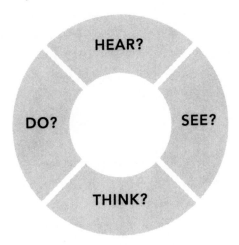

Similar to other techniques like 'customer journey mapping' and 'design thinking' the process of placing ourselves in our customer's shoes is useful to build empathy and sensitivity with customers.

For many years I was part time faculty to university and college students. The first year I taught, I remember coming home frustrated and complaining about this student who didn't do his assignments, didn't come to class and was always on his phone and disrupting the others. As a new instructor, I found it very frustrating because he was smart and talented but was not applying himself.

I will never forget what my husband said to me, "Just remember that young man is someone's son." As a new mother, it made me realize a number of things, including how important a teacher/instructor could be and how he is a person. Customers are people too.

CUSTOMER ARCHETYPES

It takes all kinds to make the world go around.

As we all know, there are many different types of customers. Professionals and trusted advisors must learn to work with and adapt to types of customers and to all of their styles. This is an art but with some skill and science, you too can master the technique of determining customer styles and customer motivations.

Customer archetypes include: Nervous Nelly who is afraid of risk and afraid to make a decision; Mousy Melanie who does what you tell her to do; Professor Paul, who secretly wants to be a professor, he needs a lot of information and loves to study it; Aggressive Andy who is difficult to stay in the room with; Know-it-All Kevin who makes you feel like you are being cross examined, thinks he is an expert and a sophisticated buyer; Silent Susan who says nothing; Negative Norman, who shoots every decision and every idea down that isn't his; Avoider Adam who will not make a decision, avoids confrontation and does not return phone calls; Chatty Cathy who won't stop talking about herself and her friends and about everyone she knows; Bully Brian; Passive Peter, who takes everyone's advice and still fails to make a conclusion or recommendation or even Obnoxious Arnold who puts off everyone he meets.

Some of us have customers like these, there are other types too, I'm sure I've missed a few.

We can help customers solve problems and offer support when we know what is keeping the customer up at night, and we know their situation, and what is happening in their world.

THE SOCIAL STYLE: OBSERVABLE BEHAVIOURS AND COMMUNICATION STYLES

In 1964, industrial psychologists Dr. David W. Merrill and Roger Reid began researching predictors of success in selling and management careers. Through empirical studies, Merrill found that people tend to display consistent, observable behaviours, and that others consistently agree on words to describe each behaviour. This work became the foundation of their SOCIAL STYLE Model™ outlined in their book, Personal Styles and Effective Performance. Like other models, it is important to recognize that it is a model: it is a guide.

Merrill and Reid, identified four social styles, each with unique language, thought processes and approaches to business. Professionals that can recognize styles and adapt their approach accordingly, can have a more productive and more harmonious working environment. Social Style Theory is based on work originated by Merrill, who used factor analysis to identify two scales, identified as assertiveness and responsiveness. This results in a model that has four quadrants, which identify four social styles. The four social styles are: Analytical, Driver, Expressive and Amiable.

As mentioned there are two scales in this model: The horizontal axis is the open emotions and closed emotions. Those that display closed emotions (drivers and analytical) display characteristics of controlled and contained emotions, are objective, reserved individuals who want facts and figures to make decisions. High responsive (expressive and amiable) are the opposite: they display emotions, they are people and relationship oriented and are subjective.

The horizontal scale is assertiveness. The far left is less assertive (analytics and amiable), they tend to ask questions and are slow to make decisions – whereas the other end assertive (drivers and expressive) tell, are assertive, and quick to make decisions.

From a building and strengthening trust point of view, each style has a different approach to how they communicate, how they make decisions, and how they are motivated. These three elements directly affect relationships of trust. When thinking about your customers ask yourself the following question: How do I adapt my style and my approach to suit the customer's preferred approach?

The following is a high level overview of what matters most to each style.

Style	What matters most	What motivates them	Most effective way to communicate
Analytical	Accuracy	Understanding and analyzing	Facts, reports, statistics, studies
Driver	Results	Excellence	Facts, to the point, agenda
Expressive	Recognition	Actions and results	Testimonials, stories, big picture
Amiable	Relationships	Consensus	People stories

Being aware of the customer's dominant style, what matters most to them, their primary motivation and have figured out the most effective way to communicate with them, allows you the opportunity to tailor your communication style to simplify the message. As we have discussed, customers make decisions to trust based on how we communicate, how we behave and how we serve.

If you are really interested in this topic, I would suggest you consider determining your own primary social style. Once you know your own style, you will be able to determine how your style affects your customers.

HIGHLIGHTS AND BEST PRACTICES FOR TRUSTED ADVISORS

- Spend five times as much time thinking about your customer and their situation as you do thinking about the project or topic on the agenda

- Determine your customer's situation

- Identify customer concerns

- Identify what value you can provide

- Find out the why

- Ask open-ended questions

- Communicate clearly

- Make recommendations that are in the best interests of the customer

- Apply the Eight Principles of Building and Protecting Trust

- Find out how you can help your customer

CASE STUDY

Meet A Trust Leader
Mary Dable Arab, District Vice President, Scotiabank

Mary Dable Arab is a wonderful example of a Trust Leader who applies and lives the trust principles every day.

Building a culture of trust and customer focus in an organization starts at the top, with the leadership team and cascades throughout the entire organization. After working with Mary and her team at Scotiabank and spending time getting to know her, I can say that Mary not only applies the trust principles, they are woven into her leadership style.

Recognized as one of Scotiabank's leaders, Mary is laser focused on creating a superior experience for customers. She is passionate about strengthening and protecting both employee trust and customer trust in the bank.

Scotiabank is Canada's most international bank and a leading financial services provider in North America, Latin America, the Caribbean and Central America and Asia-Pacific. The bank is dedicated to helping its 23 million customers become better off through a broad range of advice, products and services, including personal and commercial banking, wealth management and private banking, corporate and investment banking, and capital markets.

Mary works hard to make an impact with customers and employees every day. In her current role, Mary is responsible for leading several hundred people in branches across Nova

CASE STUDY

Scotia. She has led call centres and thousands of professionals across Canada in creating a superior customer experience for Scotiabank's customers. I sat down with Mary to find out how she does this.

Her very first sentence was: "To me, conversations about finances are very personal. We know that our customers want to work with someone they trust, and with an organization that has a good reputation. A trusted personal and corporate reputation is critical to the success of the relationship. For our customers, the person they interact with is the face of the bank. They 'are' the bank. Each person in the organization plays a key role in creating a good reputation and earning the customers' trust in Scotiabank."

With so much banking and so many transactions done online now, people do not go into the branch to "do their banking." So I asked how Scotiabank builds trust in a digital world?

"We are focused on providing an excellent customer experience in every one of the channels that our customers choose to do business with us – in a branch, online, using a mobile phone, on the telephone or at the ABM. Our guiding principle for all interactions is to make banking easier for our customers."

Mary went on to explain with a reference that I, as a mother of a teenager, could relate to well. "Kids are learning to build online apps in summer camp. They download music and games to their mobile devices in a short few clicks, and they are using the latest technology to speak with their friends and do their homework at night. These are the Scotiabank customers of the not too distant future, and we need to meet them where their needs and expectations are."

CASE STUDY

Scotiabank is committed to customer ease of use and accessibility as a practical and tangible way to demonstrate its commitment to making banking easier.

We often hear of small companies doing this successfully. And in some ways it is easier to apply the principles to a company with only a dozen employees and a few hundred customers. How does Canada's third-largest bank with over 88,000 employees and 23 million customers operationalize making it easier for its customers?

"Scotiabank is undergoing a digital transformation. We are investing in technology and automating processes to provide digital tools and solutions that better serve customers, improve speed, be more cost efficient and productive, and to be our customers' primary bank of choice. This digital transformation is what ensures we can make it effective across all of our employees and our customers."

We trust when we understand, when things are clear, when we can visualize the outcome that is being offered or described. For this reason, one of the characteristics of a trust leader is strong communications. Mary has mastered this. For example, when I asked, "What kinds of projects is Scotiabank working on as part of its digital transformation? she responded with concrete examples and visual images that helped me to understand the goal. Her language is clear and full of visual examples.

"Today, we can order and pay for a cup of coffee with our Starbucks app, and then avoid the line when we arrive to pick up our coffee. We can open an Uber account, and then order a cab and watch its progress as it arrives at our door.

Digital transformation is about identifying and reducing customer "pain points" throughout their customer journey.

CASE STUDY

Scotiabank's investments have resulted in decreases in the time it takes for customers to do their banking, including:

- The time it takes to open a day to day (chequing) account in a branch has decreased from an average of 60 minutes to less than 10 minutes.
- Further, with the launch of online account opening from Scotiabank, the ability to open an account online has decreased from approximately 15 days (with a mail in sign up package) to 3 minutes.
- The percentage of mortgage customers who can be approved in one branch visit has increased from 3 per cent to 70 per cent, and the time to complete a credit card application online has gone from about 8 minutes to about 90 seconds.

"We know that the customer experience and the customer's trust in the company are interchangeable," Mary says. "They are the brand."

A few years ago, Mary led a national project at Scotiabank to improve the customer experience. Banks continually measure customer satisfaction scores. Just before Mary returned to work after a maternity leave, she went in to see her Group Head to get up to speed. Later, Mary had a broad smile when she told me that her manager said, "Mary, we want to improve our customer satisfaction score across our Contact Centre Channels and we want you to do it. You have 18 months."

The "Oh Factor"

"I left the meeting with my baby in my arms and for the first time,

CASE STUDY

I stood outside of the bank. I thought, how do customers experience Scotiabank?" Mary studied trusted brands that were effective in delivering superior 'wow' experiences, like The Ritz Carleton, Zappos, and Disney. She found that when everyone in the organization understands their purpose, it creates a space for magic to happen. When there is clarity and simplicity around the vision, the purpose and the promise, employees are empowered to act in the customers' best interests and to 'wow' them.

Mary and her team set a goal to create positive memorable moments for Scotiabank customers, to anticipate their needs and deliver outstanding service. "I call that the 'Oh factor.' The 'Oh factor' is when you see your customer slowly say: 'Oh' and slowly smile; because you've anticipated a need they didn't even articulate." Through training and coaching, Mary and her team across the country set out to introduce the idea of Emotional Intelligence into the Customer Experience Model, as part of the effort to and increase the customer satisfaction scores in Canada and internationally.

Emotional intelligence, anticipating customer needs, and focusing on building empathy with customers were all parts of the process to create positive memorable moments for Scotiabank customers.

"When you have an anticipatory type of service, you can gain a greater sense of loyalty and customer trust and the customer will come back because you've created a positive emotional connection that is lasting." It all makes sense, so I asked for an example, again thinking how does a multinational company operationalize this?

Mary deconstructed a simple transaction that's done at the bank every day: a change of address. "Our contact centre

CASE STUDY

employees take hundreds of those calls a day. Although, what looks like an ordinary transaction may not be ordinary to you. You likely can count on one hand how many times you've moved in your lifetime. Moving can be riddled with emotion, and when we receive that customer's request to modify their profile, it's more than a transaction to us. We look for opportunities to be part of that defining moment in your life.

Despite the growth in electronic options, branches remain a vital part of banking in Canada. "Customers come into the branch to have some of the most important financial conversations of their lives," she said. "These are the 'banking moments of truth'. We have to be present and authentic and really good problem solvers." Mary and her team lead with empathy and work hard to provide their customers with an excellent customer experience."

Through emotional intelligence training and development sessions, Scotiabank employees became self-aware and adaptable, always with the goal of creating a positive memorable experience for customers. By always bringing it back to the customers and their needs, Mary and her team apply the principle of listening with empathy and compassion.

Mary and her team implemented a new Customer Experience model to over 2,000 employees in Canada. When I asked, to what do you attribute your success, she replied: "My team and I kept the customer at the centre of everything we did."

Mary has spent most of her career successfully leading large teams from 400 to 2,000 people across wide geographical footprints. "When your team is that large, you have to be very focused and your communication must be clear and grounded in passion and authenticity." According to Mary, "communication is

CASE STUDY

a competitive differentiator for leaders."

Not surprisingly, she spends a significant amount of time honing her own communication skills, preparing messages to be clear. She consistently works to improve her skills and techniques, whether it is by attending a professional development session at Harvard University or working with her team on a way to make a message come to life.

"I am committed to being as transparent and dependable as I can be in all of my interactions—both with my own team, and with the customers that we serve. When people believe you and trust you, it positively affects the outcome of all your interactions."

I could talk to Mary all day long. Her inspirational, consistent, clear and simple focus on the customer is one of the reasons Mary is recognized as a trusted leader. There is a pattern with her responses; her comments almost always mention the customer and the way that she and her team are working to improve the customer experience at Scotiabank. This passion and focus is in Mary's DNA. She is a committed, capable, consistent, compassionate and clear communicator who leads with honesty, integrity and confidence. Mary Dable Arab: A Canadian Trust Leader.

CASE STUDY

Highlights from this case study:

- Never lose sight of the customer
- Make things easy for your customer
- Always strive to create the "oh factor"
- Anticipate customer needs and what they are really asking
- Look at best practices outside of your industry
- To explain complicated concepts, use examples people can relate to
- Become aware of your emotional intelligence to build empathy
- Become a lifelong student of your craft
- Be present, put yourself in your customer's shoes
- Customer experience and customers trust are interchangeable, they are the brand

5

How Leaders Build Trust
The Eight Principles that Build, Strengthen and Protect Trust

Let's review the Eight Principles of Building, Strengthening and Protecting Trust. As you're reading through these principles, keep in mind they all work together. You can't apply just one or two principles and not the others.

1. Listen carefully with empathy and compassion, question and involve the customer or stakeholder in a dialogue
2. Communicate using clear, concrete and conversational language
3. Be honest and transparent
4. Be consistent, predictable and reliable
5. Act in the best interests of customers, stakeholders and the public
6. Do the right thing. If you make a mistake fix it
7. Deliver on your promise
8. Commit to the long term

The Eight Principles are at the heart of a customer's decision to trust your company.

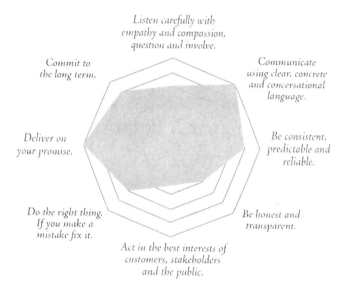

Listen carefully with empathy and compassion, question and involve.

Commit to the long term.

Communicate using clear, concrete and conversational language.

Deliver on your promise.

Be consistent, predictable and reliable.

Do the right thing. If you make a mistake fix it.

Be honest and transparent.

Act in the best interests of customers, stakeholders and the public.

The companies and the leaders that have high trust with their customers, suppliers, employees and stakeholders, apply all of the principles. When you conduct yourself according to these principles, you will build, strengthen and protect relationships of trust. And it's not just about applying these principles with customers. Successful professionals apply these principles to everything they do.

Whether we are making a personal decision or a business decision, we use the same decision making process. People buy from people they trust, people they feel good about, people they can relate to and people they respect.

As mentioned in the previous chapter, these principles were tested in various environments. Through multiple testing including correlation and factor analysis, and peer reviewed research, the following Eight Principles are the questions customers are asking when they are deciding to trust a company.

Principle 1

Listen Carefully, with Empathy and Compassion, Question and Involve the Customer or Stakeholder in a Dialogue

People like to talk about themselves. Think about your last customer meeting. Who did most of the talking?

Some time ago, a friend invited me to join her and a colleague, who we will call Paula, for lunch. She told me ahead of time that she wanted me to meet this coworker, as Paula was interested in learning ways to build and improve trust with their members. I appreciated the introduction and did my homework. I read the annual report, their website and talked to a few of their stakeholders. I was prepared to ask several exploratory questions. But before we even sat down, Paula started talking. For 90 minutes straight, she talked about her background, the organization, people, her challenges, her woes and what she does for fun.

A few hours after the lunch, my friend called to say, "Paula was so impressed with you. She said it was the best meeting she has had in months and will be in touch, as they would like to move to the next stage."

If someone from another table had been observing us, it would have looked like the woman was telling me the story of her life. She was talking "at me" the entire time. As the old saying goes, "I did not get a word in edgewise." My friend told me Paula felt great.

People respond positively when they do most of the talking and the focus is on them. We are happy when other people listen to us, whether it is face to face, over the telephone, on even on social media. The more you listen, the greater the impact.

Harvard neuroscientist Jason Mitchell and physiology graduate student Diana Tamir found that self-disclosure activates the same regions of the brain as sex, money and food. Their 2012 research, revealed about 40 per cent of our everyday speech is devoted to telling others how we think or feel about something. According to Mitchell, "We will often go to comic lengths to avoid talking about others and to keep the focus on us."

There are three key elements of listening: sincerity, curiosity and genuine interest. Adopting all three can have a positive impact on your business.

Most of us think we are good listeners. If you ask whether they're good listeners, most people will say yes. Companies think they are good listeners too. But the reality is that most of us are not good listeners. The good news: it's a skill that can be learned. The ability to listen well will affect your success in life. It also affects the bottom line. Listening is a critical step to connecting with a customer or colleague and to building a relationship of trust.

LISTENING: A LEADERSHIP TRUST BUILDING AND TRUST PROTECTING TOOL

In their Harvard Business Review article "Listening to People," authors Dr. Ralph G. Nichols and Leonard A. Stevens make the case that if business people were taught how to listen, business would benefit. After performing in-depth interviews with executives in a manufacturing plant, they concluded that people do not know how to listen. To be a good listener, one must apply specific skills. This article was published in 1957, however their findings are still relevant today.

In their classic book, Are you Listening? authors Nichols and Stevens refer to studies done at the University of Minnesota with thousands of students. The tests led to the general conclusion that, "Immediately after the average person has listened to someone talk, he remembers only about half of what he has heard — no matter how carefully he thought he was listening."

Scientists have been researching memory and the capacity of the human brain for years. Basically, they found that the brain's excess capacity takes over when we listen to others, and we end up thinking about other things. Additionally, studies show that the average human attention span is less than a goldfish. In the year 2000, or around the time the mobile revolution began, the average attention span was 12 seconds. It is now eight seconds, as reported by Leon Watson in United Kingdom's Telegraph newspaper on May 15, 2015. The study, conducted by Microsoft in 2015, surveyed 2,000 participants in Canada and studied the brain activity of 112 others using electroencephalograms.

By the way, it is believed the goldfish has an attention span of nine seconds. No wonder listening is a lost art.

One may say the need to teach good listening skills is more important now than it was 60 years ago. It also supports what we will look at in Principle #2: Communicate with Clear Concrete and Conversational Language. If we only have eight seconds, the message better be clear or it won't be processed. A general rule of thumb is to keep it simple, and to convey only one point or one message when responding to a question.

"The effectiveness of the spoken word hinges not so much on how people talk, as on how they listen," say Nichols and Stevens. When we communicate, we want the listener to understand our ideas. Good listeners focus on grasping ideas.

EMOTIONS FILTER MESSAGES

Listening is affected by our emotions, and emotions are key to the trust decision. Emotions lurk in every crevasse of the human organism. They are present in everything we do and experience. Our emotions filter the messages we hear, hence the expression, "We hear what we want to hear." When we hear things that oppose our beliefs or views, or upset us, it over-stimulates the brain because we are thinking of a response. Many years ago I sat on a management team with a vice president who started his response to every question with, "That won't work because..." or "We can't do this because..." or "We do not have the resources to..." After a few meetings, he was unofficially labeled "An idea buster" and some people stopped sharing new ideas with him.

Conversely, when we hear things that support our ideas, views and beliefs, mental barriers are dropped and messages are welcomed. We tend to listen to the entire idea or message. For example, if you hear the proposal you sent to a potential customer is "Bang on track with the company's objectives," you will continue to listen intently for more details and feedback. But if you hear "The proposal missed the mark," your focus might well shift to "What or how did this happen?" or "Where was the disconnect?"

What can we do about this emotional filter? One way is to concentrate on re-serving judgment until after the speaker is finished.

When discussing listening and the impact of listening without emotion and judgment, I often show workshop and seminar participants a quote from Indian Philosopher Jiddu Krishnamurti:

> "If you are listening to find out, then your mind is free, not committed to anything; it is very acute, sharp, alive, inquiring, curious and therefore capable of discovery."

An Edelman survey in 2017 found 53 per cent of people do not regularly listen to people or organizations with whom they often disagree. People are nearly four times more likely to ignore information that supports a position they do not believe in.

Businesses need to listen and gather objective customer insights. Listening without bias, without emotional filters, involves obtaining objective customer feedback. Companies sometimes do this by hiring a third party objective researcher.

We trust people we are comfortable with. We are comfortable with people we trust, admire, respect, like, feel good about, feel safe with and can relate to. Familiarity is established primarily through listening and dialogue. Dialogue enables familiarity and the opportunity to develop a connection. Establishing connections and familiarity lead to likeability. Studies have shown that feelings of trust are related to confidence and likeability.

UNDERSTAND WHAT IS IMPORTANT TO YOUR CUSTOMERS

It's important for organizations to understand their customers. What is important to them? What are they interested in? Understanding starts with listening and building trust begins with the intention of understanding. Mutual understanding strengthens trust. When customers understand an organization, they are more likely to buy into its goals.

Empathic listening demonstrates respect. Examples of empathy include: taking customers into consideration when making a decision, walking a mile in a customer's shoes, trying to understand their needs, and looking at the world from their point of view. Asking questions, encouraging employee participation and involving stakeholders through dialogue can cultivate relationships. Public relations expert Dr. Sandra C. Duhé says, "Effective stakeholder engagement involves seeking input from even those voices corporations may rather not, but need to hear." People expect organizations to actively engage with them and to listen to them. Customers become turned off from organizations that fail to actively engage or listen. People have choices. They want to do business with people and organizations that listen.

As businessman and author Stephen Covey said, "Seek first to understand, then to be understood." When individuals are comfortable and feel safe, they share information.

LISTENING IN BUSINESS

Do you listen carefully enough? Are you demonstrating enough empathy and compassion with your customers?

I have a client, a digital media company that thought of itself as a company that listened. They thought they understood what was important to their customers. The head of business development said, "We talk to customers all the time." But as we have established, talking and listening are not the same thing. They are very different. When we conducted the Client Trust Index™ on this company, the agency scored very low in the Listening with Empathy principle. Their customers said they did not understand their business. The company didn't realize it at the time, but they were losing customers because of it.

What about your organization? Are you losing business because you're not listening to your customers?

One simple way to demonstrate you are listening is to repeat what the person said or to paraphrase. Think about the last time you went through a drive-thru for coffee. You drive up to the first audio box, place your order and the attendant says, "That will be $2.45. Please drive up to the next window." You get to the window and the attendant says, "Medium black coffee?" They repeat your order. They are showing you that they are listening. If you go inside to the counter, the same thing happens. Try it. As you will see, they are repeating to show you they are listening and to confirm they have the order right.

Listening becomes impactful when we add empathy. Empathy means understanding someone's situation, being sensitive to and aware of their emotional thoughts and feelings. When we listen with empathy we actively try to understand the other person's point of view.

When you are listening with empathy you are actively sensing another person's situation, including:

+ Feelings
+ Non-verbal cues
+ Concerns
+ Tone
+ Awareness of implications

After you have processed the information the person shares with you, here are a few ways you can respond to demonstrate empathy:

1. Display assurances that make sense, say "I understand your point of view"
2. Ask questions to further understand
3. Display body language that shows you are listening. For example, nod your head at a slow pace, show concentration in your facial expression, look at the person who is speaking and do not appear rushed or in a hurry. Show patience.
4. Paraphrase what the other person has said
5. Verbal probes, for example, "ah ha," "yes," "got it," " I am following you," and "I understand."

COMPASSION AND NEUROSCIENCE

Empathy and compassion are closely related, yet there is a difference between them. Compassion is about feelings and being sympathetic to the other's situation and wanting to help them, where empathy is more rational. It is about understanding the situation from the other person's perspective, including their emotions.

According to the University of California, Berkley Greater Good Science Center, "Compassion literally means to suffer together. Among emotion researchers, it is defined as the feeling that arises when you are confronted with another's suffering and feel motivated to relieve that suffering."

This research has shown that when we feel compassion, our heart rate slows down and regions of the brain that are linked to caregiving, such as feelings of pleasure and empathy, will light up. Also, the peptide hormone oxytocin is released when you show another person that you care, or demonstrate compassion. Maybe this is why American neuroeconomist Paul Zak of Claremont Graduate University calls oxytocin "the moral molecule." There is a lot of data that suggest we are wired to care, down to the neurochemical level.

BE COMPASSIONATE IN BUSINESS

Sometimes it's tough being the boss. You often have to make difficult decisions that will leave people feeling upset. If you have to lay off an employee, for example, you need to think about the impact it will have on their life. It will affect not only their status and income, but also their ego. You can demonstrate compassion to try to help them with their situation. Maybe you do this by offering severance or work placement consulting services to help them find a new job. You do this because you have sympathy and want to help them with their situation. Put yourself in their position. Think about how you would feel and be compassionate. When we listen, understand a situation and show compassion, we get more positive results. We can show compassion in little acts every single day.

Anthropology professor Dr. David Buss of Tufts University generated a lot of controversy when he surveyed 10,000 people from 37 different countries — heterosexuals at the age of forming romantic partnerships — and asked them: What is most important to you in a mate? Gender differences generated all the attention around this remarkable study. Women were a bit more interested in men's financial prospects than men were in women's, so according to this study, women value resources a little more. And men were a bit more interested in women's beauty than women were in men's looks.

But there was another result that no one talked about: kindness was found to be the most important criterion for a mate, and the single universal requirement across these 37 countries. People are looking for kindness as a mating strategy. You might be asking yourself what does this have to do with business?

> Customers are people; they want to do business with kind compassionate companies and kind, compassionate people.

The medical profession has been attuned to the science of empathy and compassion for generations. Empirical studies in the medical profession have found that when doctors are empathic and compassionate during a consultation, it leads to decreased patient anxiety and more positive health outcomes.

In May 2015, I met one of Australia's health care communications scholars, Dr. Bernadette Watson, at the International Communication Association conference in San Juan, Puerto Rico. She presented findings from a recent research study she and Dr. Susan C. Baker conducted with 103 patients in Australia. The study demonstrated that "Perceptions of Care and Compassion Matter."

When a physician demonstrates compassion, patients become more willing to communicate and share information.

How does this relate to business? If your company shows compassion and empathy, your customers will share more information with you. For a doctor, a patient is usually more comfortable communicating and taking the prescribed treatment;

in the business world, the customer is more willing to take your recommendation, advice or move forward with you.

THE PHYSICIAN'S TECHNIQUE

My experience has been that doctors are generally good listeners, even if they are extremely busy and only have 10 minutes for you. They ask you how things are going, they don't interrupt you, they ask questions to clarify and wait until you are finished before they say, "Okay, let's take a look." They ask questions to fully understand your situation, so they can give diagnoses.

Here is a simple example: a patient shows up at a doctor's office with a skin rash. After the preliminaries, the doctor will ask a series of questions that may go something like this:

+ How long have you had the problem?
+ Where were you on that day?
+ Have you had anything different to eat?
+ Did you encounter any animals or plants?
+ Has it spread?
+ Is it itchy?
+ Is it hot?
+ Does water bother it?
+ Have you put anything on it?
+ Does anyone else in the house have it?

I am not a doctor, however I recognize their technique. They listen with genuine curiosity. They are usually empathetic and take the time to understand the situation. The good doctors are compassionate and many sincerely care. Their intent is to holistically understand and to help. When your intention is to understand, you are not passing judgment.

My mother is a nurse. When I am out with her, people often tell her their health issues. For example, we were at a restaurant together on a busy Saturday waiting for a table and a woman that my mother knew from church came over to say hello. Within minutes she started telling my mother about her chipped tooth and her knee issues. My mother said that happens all the time. I know from experience that she is a good listener. She makes people feel comfortable, safe and her intention is to understand the situation.

The business world is recognizing this as well. In January 2016, Fast Company Magazine published its 20 predictions for the next 20 years — Trend #12: Human Empathy will be Central. Professionals who become masters at empathizing with people will stand out and become more valuable to customers. We want to do business with people who understand us, "get" us, appreciate us, and understand our world.

ENGAGING AND COLLABORATING

Once you have mastered the skill of listening with empathy and compassion, next comes questioning and involving your customer in a dialogue.

Journalists and talk show hosts are often good listeners, as they are naturally curious. They are trained to listen for all the facts. Consider television talk show host Ellen DeGeneres. When you watch her, you can see that she lets the other person finish their statement before she responds, and she leans in to the other speaker to show she is listening.

The process of questioning and engaging in dialogue enhances mutual understanding, connectivity, awareness and collaboration. When we are involved in a discussion and feel part of it, we are more committed. When an organization listens to its customers before making decisions that affect them, it builds trust. Virgin America is an example of an organization that successfully does this. In a survey, Virgin America asked its customers what type of food they would like served on long flights. Customers responded and they built a specific menu around the findings.

Organizations with more technical and scientifically based products will often hold user conferences and scientific roundtables with stakeholders to engage and collaborate. When I was the manager of market activation at Computer Sciences Corporation for the financial services division, we held what we called CUSUGA every fall for many years. CUSUGA stood for Computer Sciences User Group Association. During the three or four day event we would have an opportunity to learn about customer issues, their business and upcoming plans. We would also have an opportunity to share, collaborate with them and inform them of our plans. This mutual understanding and reciprocity builds trust. We would return with new product and development ideas, and new ways of doing things. We also hosted smaller events, customers advisory board meetings with only 20 to 30 people at a time. Events like these strengthen mutual understanding and foster reciprocity.

Many companies host business reviews with customers, dinners or socials, to keep each other up to date. It is an effective way to listen and engage with customers and to meet with stakeholders face to face. Polls, surveys, focus groups, online chat groups can also be effective for listening and understanding a customer's situation, and to gain feedback.

BODY LANGUAGE THAT TELLS CUSTOMERS YOU ARE LISTENING

Have you ever gone to a networking event, and while you are talking to someone they were looking over your shoulder to see who else is in the room? When this happens, as it has to me, it doesn't feel very good. It tells you that you are not as important as others, and that the person isn't listening to you. This body language erodes trust.

Several books, posts and articles have been written about body language. Videos, presentations and TED talks galore focus on body language. It is a huge subject that we continue to learn about every day. Body language accounts for more than half the message you are sending out. When you first meet someone, more than 50 per cent of what they respond to and use as the basis of judgment about you is based on body language. By becoming aware of the message you are sending out, you can be 50 per cent ahead of the game.

As body language relates to listening, we need to ask ourselves what signals and messages are we sending others, and what feedback are we sending in response to the signals they are sending to us?

To demonstrate listening, pay attention to:

- Body movement - Sitting or standing still, with little movement communicates listening. Control and limit body movements. For example, a slow nod of the head shows you are listening
- Tone of voice – Keep your tone calm and controlled
- Pace of voice. Talking too quickly can communicate you are rushed, impatient and not hearing what the other person is saying
- Keep your facial expression open and curious. When you frown, it could imply you are judging what they are saying and not listening
- Position your body toward the speaker or speakers
- Lean forward slightly when the other person is speaking

LISTENING AND ASKING FOR FEEDBACK

We hear many reasons from companies as to why they do not want to assess their customer's trust in them including, "We have a great reputation," "Clients love us," "I know what our clients would say," "Our customers are happy," "We don't want to hear the complainers." It is important to note that these responses do not correspond with trust. Listening to customers is critical. Asking for customer feedback in a way that it is anonymous and non-confrontational is critical.

Most customers do not like confrontation, nor do they to complain. According to F1 Financial Training Services, 96 per cent of unhappy customers do not complain. And of the 96 per cent of unhappy customers who do not complain, 91 per cent will leave and never come back. After 10 years, we switched our family dentist. We were not happy with the lack of service, we did not complain, we left and will not go back to him. After four years of poor service from our accountant, we left without complaining and will not use his services again. I'm sure you have had similar experiences in your own life.

Customers are more likely to defect to the competition if they are having a service-related problem, rather than price or product related. How we serve often starts with listening carefully with empathy and compassion, questioning and involving customers in a conversation.

Seven Steps to Communicating with Empathy

1. Listen carefully when you are being asked a question

2. Respect every question no matter how trite it may seem

3. Ask clarification questions and take notes when appropriate

4. Pause for two or three seconds before you begin your response. When you begin to speak, speak slowly. As we have discussed, calm, careful listening and patience projects professionalism, confidence and respect.

5. Acknowledge the concern behind their statement, question or opinion. Empathize with the customer on the importance of the issue.

    Dr. Harvey Karp author of "The Happiest Toddler on the Block," says when a parent acknowledges a child's concern, it defuses the situation. The child immediately feels they are being heard. Someone has listened to them.

    This translates directly to the business world. If an organization says, "We are raising our prices" and customers raise concerns, the company can defuse the situation by responding with, "We understand you are concerned and respect your point of view."

6. Give an example of how to demonstrate that you personally understand the importance of an issue. Share a personal experience related to your own background. Remember people like to talk about themselves, not you, so keep this to a minimum so the focus stays on the customer.

7. Answer the question in a factual way as it relates to your general expertise. This will demonstrate you are not being judgemental.

BUILDING TRUST AND NEGOTIATING UNDER PRESSURE STARTS WITH LISTENING

Advice from a Former Chief Negotiator
Royal Canadian Mounted Police

Bill Brydon spent 32 years with the Royal Canadian Mounted Police (RCMP). As the leader of the RCMP's Crisis Negotiator Team in Nova Scotia, Canada he mastered the art of building trust under pressure. In this role he trained other police officers to peacefully resolve life and death situations. Most of the time he negotiated over the phone or through a loud hailer.

Although business negotiations are usually much different in tone and outcome, these lessons are never the less important for business leaders. Brydon's approach to negotiating starts with assessing and listening. This approach leads to building trust. Here are some of his guidelines:

"Understand the situation before you begin negotiations."
When Brydon was called the risks were high, therefore current and accurate information was needed to assess the situation. Using an extensive questionnaire he sought information that he could use to assist him in building trust.

"Keep your mouth shut and your ears open"
Brydon demonstrated with actual examples how much we can learn when we actively listen. We listened to a recording of a hostage negotiation together. During the initial 90-second exchange Brydon spoke less than 10 words, however he learned the hostage takers motivation, who else was in the building, what the hostage meant to him and what his short and long term needs were. Further, he learned the subject had a racial bias, did not like the government and did not trust the police.

Brydon's objective was to apply the active listening skills of emotional labeling, paraphrasing, mirroring, and "I" messages to help control the emotion, earn trust and end the situation without anyone getting hurt.

Focus
Brydon has negotiated from cars, sheds, houses and outdoors in extreme Canadian weather. Negotiators need to be skilled at tuning out external influences and focus on the person being spoken to, making sure they know they are important and valued.

Master the art of the open-ended question
Brydon routinely asked questions that could not be answered with a simple yes or no answer. He wants people to talk. When I listened to one of Brydon's recorded calls in a hostage situation, he started with one of his favourite questions, "How is everybody doing?" followed by, "What is going on in there?"

When the negotiation breaks down, start over
A crisis negotiator knows that there is a natural process to the negotiation and you cannot skip steps. When the negotiation stumbles you have to go back to the last step that you were successful at and start over.

When asked what advice Brydon would give a seasoned negotiator with 10 – 20 years experience, he said, "**Never stop learning.**" He then recounted a story of a role-play situation where the actor knew right away that the negotiator (with 15 years experience) was not taking her seriously. The negotiator was slumped in her chair, displayed an uncaring attitude and the actor was able to sense the disinterest over the phone. Crisis negotiators have to be 100% engaged, as it could be the difference between ending or saving lives.

Now, as the Director of Operations for Commissionaires Nova Scotia, Brydon applies the skills he learned as a crisis negotiator to the business environment.

Key Takeaways:

- Customers love talking about themselves and love it when people listen to them

- Listening is a form of respect

- Emotions lurk in every crevasse of the human organism, check your emotional listening filters

- We hear what we want to hear

- The way you listen in any given moment can either build or destroy trust

- Mutual understanding and empathy strengthen relationships of trust

- Engaging in dialogue and collaborating engenders trust

10 Questions to ask yourself about you and your company

1. Do you listen in a way that would encourage customers or colleagues to talk freely?

2. When controversial topics come up do you:
   a. Ask questions for clarification?
   b. Request more information? or
   c. Ask for time to check facts before passing judgment?

3. What emotional filters do you and your company have? How can you manage those?

4. How many clarification questions do you ask customers to learn about their situation?

5. How do you demonstrate empathy?

6. How frequent do you engage with customers and stakeholders?

7. How do you display compassion? Does everyone display it?

8. Do you ask questions to understand your customer's situation? Do you and your customers share a mutual understanding? Do you understand each other?

9. Have you asked your customers for feedback on your listening ability?

10. Do you collaborate and involve your customers in discussions that affect them?

Principle 2

Communicate Using Clear, Concrete and Conversational Language

Clarity inspires trust. Put simply, we trust what we believe and what we understand. If we do not understand a message, we are inclined to distrust it. We're less likely to trust when a message is vague, complex, incomprehensible or filled with jargon. Being wishy-washy inhibits credibility, which inhibits trust. Communication applies to the written, verbal, vocal and visual messages that your organization is communicating.

> *"Simple can be harder than complex: You have to work hard to get your thinking clean to make it simple. But it's worth it in the end because once you get there, you can move mountains."*
>
> - Steve Jobs

Organizations should strive to be clear in all types of their communication, including:

1. Their purpose, vision and objectives
2. Organizational messages such as policies, processes, products and procedures
3. Expectations
4. Everyday interactions

As we discussed in the chapter on hidden assets, when an organization can clearly articulate its purpose, vision and objectives, it can "move mountains." This is the first step to building a customer centered trust culture. Without a clear plan, that is shared, people do not know what to do, why they are doing it, or where they're doing it and with whom. Plans inspire clarity.

ORGANIZATIONAL MESSAGES AND EXPECTATIONS

From a company's website, to policies, to the annual report, the signage and the product literature, corporate messages must be communicated in a clear, specific, believable and conversational format. Vague language and generalities often force us to fill in the blanks. The more specific you can be, the better.

Here are some indicators that might suggest you need to improve in this area:

✓ Customers are asking the same questions repeatedly

✓ Customers are asking for instructions or clarification about a particular product, service or policy

✓ Customers ask, "Is there any other information you can send us?"

✓ Customers say, "We need an engineer/lawyer/computer scientist/ accountant/doctor/or other specialist to understand this!" or "Can you explain this in plain language?"

✓ Customers say, "We need further details. Can you send us a diagram or the outline of each phase?"

✓ Customers do not understand your policies

✓ Sales cycles are long and or you do not have a high ratio of closes for the number of sales calls

✓ Negotiations take longer than they should

These are just examples and every situation is different. You might be dealing with a customer that needs more time to make a decision or to get to know the company. Sometimes, people use questions as a stall tactic so they can delay making a decision.

When you're hearing employees say things like "This is the first I heard of this," or every employee says the company does something different or describes it in a different way, that's an indicator that the organization's culture does not support clear communication.

Companies should not use large complicated words or vagueness when describing themselves. One company I know describes itself as "a paradigm changer in the knowledge economy." I have no idea what they do from this statement. They say they are an information technology company with training products for knowledge workers, but what does that mean? I have asked them for examples of projects they have worked on; they offered complication stories in response. I have even requested a more specific description from the CEO, sales manager, director of marketing and manager of delivery, and they all say something a little different. In this situation, it is impossible for me to refer customers to them, as I can't explain what they do.

When people ask me about Success Through Trust, I do not say to them, "I'm all about trust," because that's not a clear message. People do not understand that. I share with them that I work with companies to build customer commitment, loyalty and increase profits. Then when they ask me how I do that, I tell them I offer seminars, online courses, and books on building trust with customers, assess and measure customer's trust in a company, and I show people how to apply the principles of building trust to improve their businesses.

Of course I tailor each message to an individual customer's situation. For example, if they have issues within their organization, then I would help them build trust internally. Customer trust is always a focus. In some ways, being a customer-focused organization has become a lost art. I help organizations focus on the customer and acting in the customer's best interests.

> We feel confident when we understand what's happening around us. When we don't understand, we tend to glaze over and distrust. Confidence, clarity and simplicity inspire trust. Organizations should strive to communicate in simple everyday language that customers and stakeholders understand.

As economics and business scholar Gilbert W. Fairholm said in his 1994 book Leadership and the Culture of Trust, "Trust is increased by the acquisition of more true knowledge." Sharing of information, dialogue and communicating on a regular basis contributes to building trust. When organizations consistently provide clear, concrete and concise messages, in a conversational tone trust is created and strengthened. When we understand, we are more likely to buy into the goals of an organization.

Even colours can communicate your message. For example, blue is well known as a colour that represents trust, honesty, loyalty, dependability and strength. Think of the companies you know that use blue: IBM, Wal-Mart, Costco, OralB, Vimeo, Dell, AT&T, Bell, Twitter, Facebook, Oreo, American Express, General Electric, Ocean Spray and WestJet are just a few.

As discussed in previous chapters, when employees work in an empowering environment, they act like owners. The same goes for customers. When customers are empowered they will feel and act like partners. Customers need to be aware and understand to be empowered. People like to be part of something.

Tactically speaking, there are several ways to effectively communicate with customers, including making reliable, trustworthy information available via: scientific papers, whitepapers, magazines, newsletters from respected authorities, industry information, meeting briefings. Or there are online options: social media, personalized notes from the CEO or senior management team. Storytelling is a powerful way to share and transfer messages. Choose your own best option but keep the message clear and simple. This is critical to your success.

GUIDELINES TO COMMUNICATING WITH GREATER CLARITY AND CREDIBILITY

What we say must be clear, concise and credible. We trust what we believe and what we understand. Long-winded explanations, detailed descriptions, and complex arguments confuse customers and often can project evasion, fuzzy thinking and disorganization to the customer or prospect.

You can communicate with greater clarity by following these nine guidelines:

1. Simplify your point

A banking executive gives us a good example of how to simplify small business bank financing: "Banks are in the business of providing low risk financing. Our margins are not exactly huge. It just takes one or two bad loans to wipe out the profits on a hundred good ones. That's why small businesses have a hard time getting start up financing from banks."

2. Avoid vague generations and platitudes. Be specific

Do not say: "We are augmenting our service offering with the strategic introduction of some popular IT security products."

Do Say: "Next month we are going to start selling Internet security products for smart phones, laptops and tablets."

3. Use concrete, familiar words

Eliminate, as much as you can, adjectives, qualifiers, buzzwords, acronyms, jargon and abstract terms.

The average person's reading vocabulary ranges from 25,000 to 50,000 words, but their speaking vocabulary, the words they are most comfortable with, contains fewer than 10,000. Follow the example of newscasters who confine themselves to a vocabulary range of fewer than 7,000 words.

Do not say, as the telephone executive did: "Careful operationalization of this policy is needed in order to avoid the pitfall of goal displacement."
Do Say: "We must follow this policy if we want to meet our sales quota."

4. Make only one strong point in response to each question

Do not try to squeeze in two or three points or too much information particularly, in conversation. The more you say, the less people will remember.

5. Support your points with examples

Good examples can capture attention, explain and enhance credibility more effectively than any other communications technique. Ronald Reagan's mastery of the technique of communicating with examples earned him the title The Great Communicator. The former President responded to almost every difficult media question by saying, "Let me tell you a story," and he would tell one, often with personal details. The stories simplified his message so that everyone could understand it.

When you need to communicate with your customers and stakeholders, ask yourself, "What example or story will clarify this point?"
Examples can:

- Relate your point directly to the customer's day-to-day experience

- Make messages easy to visualize. 55 per cent of people are visual learners. Cold facts and abstract statements are not easy to visualize
- Associate you with values, individuals, other customers, individuals, places, situations that enhance your credibility.

Draw examples from personal experiences, things that happened to someone you know or heard about, history, something in the news, or a famous person's life. They can be humorous or serious. They can even be hypothetical: "Imagine how you would feel if..."

Build a file of examples that support the messages you want to communicate. Practice relating those examples to your friends and colleagues until they become part of your mental inventory, ready to be recalled when you are given an opportunity.

Examples are often remembered long after your other messages are forgotten.

6. Use simple numbers and statistics, not many

People trust numbers. We accept numbers as facts. Numbers can simplify, clarify and convince. But use them sparingly; too many numbers can confuse. Limit the numbers and statistics you use to two or three in each message. Convert large numbers into simple percentages to round them off.

"The advertising costs only amount to three cents to every sales dollar."

"30 per cent of every dollar that comes in the door is being lost to inefficiency."

"Last year we spent $400,000 retraining our employees. That's an average of $3,000 for every person on our payroll."

7. Divide your message into three parts

Effective communicators often clarify some of their messages by breaking them into three parts. This technique allows you to quickly organize and simplify responses to broad and complex questions so that customers and stakeholders will understand and pay more attention to them.

There is something logical and compelling about the number three. Two is not quite enough and four is usually one more than you need. That is why we have Three Wise Men, Three Musketeers, Three Elements of Trust, Three dimensions of Trust and so on.

✓ Point out three challenges facing the organization
✓ Give three reasons for supporting the decision
✓ Cite three features of the product
✓ Present three choices for consideration
✓ Propose three initiatives
✓ Plan three phases
✓ Describe three advantages to the plan
✓ List three priorities for next year
✓ Make three important points

You may ask, what if there are more than three? You can still use this technique by saying: "Three priorities, challenges, opportunities etc.," "I want to mention three points" or "The three most important issues are…"

Now that you are aware of this technique, you will be surprised how often you notice it being used. Hundreds of our seminar participants will attest to its effectiveness.

8. Use appropriate metaphors, images and videos

Metaphors are a great way to package a message and make it clearer for customers to understand your message. They provide comparisons and visuals. Pay attention and make sure that the metaphors you choose send messages that are aligned with the visuals and make the right comparisons with you and your organization.

For example: Sue is as excited as a kid in a candy store – Sue is upbeat

Remember, 55 per cent of the population is visual, so clearly images are import-ant when conveying your trust messages.

Images can help simplify, help explain and help us remember points. Images can include, charts, info graphics, pictures, and conventional graphics. As the saying goes. "A picture tells 1000 words." Simple videos can be powerful as well.

9. Support your points with facts and quote independent authorities

Projecting credibility begins with telling the truth. Having said this, you can add credibility to your messages and your responses to customer questions if you follow these two guidelines.

1. Support your points with facts
2. Quote independent authorities

You strengthen your credibility when you support your points with information and opinions obtained from independent sources and respected authorities. Avoid offering an opinion when you can cite a fact that will make the point for you. People can argue with an opinion. They cannot argue with a fact.

In addition to these guidelines, the following phrases and words can inspire or destroy trust.

Phrases that Inspire Trust

+ "I will take care of this"
+ "Tell me more"
+ "Can you tell me about that"

- "We do not do that, we will find you a company that does."
- "I don't know."
- "I do not know how to do that."
- "That makes sense."
- "Take your time"
- "Thank you"

Words that build, strengthen and protect trust

Warranty	Exposure
Guarantee	Leakage
Certified	Vulnerabilities
Strengthen	Trap
Build	Cover up
Open	Violate
Transparency	Risk assurance
Rigorous	Dark horse
Innovation	Hazard
Creative	Problem
Accountability	Risk
Ethics	Profit – "we have to make a profit"
Money back	Here are the conditions
Threat	To be honest with you
Fraud	Fine print
Litigation	Sign here
Compromise	Let me be frank

KOHLTECH INTERNATIONAL
A TRUST LEADER IN COMMUNICATIONS

Kohltech International is an example of a Canadian manufacturing company whose communication is clear, concrete and concise. Kohltech makes windows and entrance systems. From their website to the manufacturing facility, to their clean trucks with professional images, to the product, the message is clear: Kohltech builds high quality windows and doors.

Their website is beautifully designed and easy to use. You can find a dealer or watch a video to see the plant where the windows are manufactured. The company is accessible and empowers its customers with information.

Their physical presence communicates trust. When you drive into the parking lot of the corporate offices you'll notice a large sign on the building, visible signage for parking, and the area is professionally landscaped. Inside the foyer, you are greeted with a smile and acknowledgement that you are expected. Like many offices, there is a visitor book to sign in and there is a nice waiting area with comfortable seating. Kohltech International's promise, vision, and creed are prominently displayed on the walls in their offices throughout the plant, as well as on their website. Their vision is to be North America's most respected window and door company, and their promise is to be outstanding. Everything they do communicates "outstanding."

According to a 2009 global survey conducted by the Edelman Trust Barometer, people need to hear information about a company three to five times in order to believe the information. Clear, concise messages should be regularly repeated.

13 Simple ways to audit your company's communication for clarity and simplicity

1. Publish and post the company purpose and objectives where employees can see them.

2. Ask yourself whether your messages answer the questions customers are asking.

3. Communicate company policies to your customers.

4. Seek feedback to determine if your customers clearly understand your policies and processes.

5. Do new customers know how you work? Do they know what is expected of them as customers?

6. Are customer expectations in line with what you are offering?

7. Identify frequently asked questions (FAQs) that customers, partners, suppliers or stakeholders ask. Are they written down? Are they easily accessible?

8. Outline agreements in one or two pages. For example, review your support, warranty, customer contracts, and return policies. Do you avoid fine print and cumbersome contracts?

9. Check the vocabulary. Would your uncle understand it? Would a glossary of terms be helpful

10. Avoid acronyms.

11. Do messages incorporate elements for visual, auditory and kinesthetic learners? Items may include visuals, pictures and diagrams for the visual learners? Do they incorporate demonstrations or surveys for kinesthetic learners?

12. Experience your company from your customer's point of view. When they interact with you, are the messages clear?

13. Audit all collateral, signage and marketing materials to ensure the branding and messaging is consistent. Items may include videos, whitepapers, podcasts, advertisements, blog posts, email signature lines, company photos, trade show booths, social media sites and the uniforms employees wear.

Principle 3

Be Honest and Transparent

Telling the truth is not a new idea. Your grandmother might have told you that "nothing builds trust like the truth," or what Benjamin Franklin said; "Honesty is the best policy."

This is especially true in business. Scott McCain, Director of McCain Foods, which produces a third of the world's French fries and is one of the world's largest producers of frozen foods, and President JSM Capital Corp. says, "*One of the most important values is to dare to be transparent. People are people, they will give you a mulligan. Try to let people know the honest truth, admit mistakes, let people know you are trying to do your best. Be accountable, do not blame anybody but ourselves, and keep everyone informed every step of the way. If you don't know the answer, be honest, and tell people, we don't know but we are going to find out. It is a fine line. It takes courage and confidence to be open, honest and transparent.*"

Dean Robertson, President and CEO of The Shaw Group also advises leaders to be open: "be upfront in your communications, share as much information as you can with your employees, clients and your partners."

But not every company is ready to follow the advice of Franklin and your grandmother. Toronto Star journalist David Olive reported that the Takata Corporation airbag recall was the biggest consumer product recall in history, in his 2015 article *Five painful lessons from the Takata airbag recall*. Approximately 34 million airbags made by Takata in Japan had to be recalled and replaced. The malfunctioning airbags were linked to seventeen deaths, mostly in the U.S. The Takata airbags exploded, shooting metal shards into the bodies of drivers and passengers. Olive's article included information about the complexity of the supply chain process, myths about the quality brand, fines and government involvement.

Olive concluded that "Business lies," describing business in general as "like a cheap broadloom. It lies until an energetic regulator, media expose or class action lawsuit forces the truth out of a recalcitrant company."

That is a pretty harsh assessment. But a lot has been written about the business case for treachery. Professors Amar Bhide and Howard H. Stevenson wrote an article in the Harvard Business Review asking "Why be Honest if Honesty Doesn't Pay?" After reviewing case studies and conducting interviews, they concluded, "Business men and women keep their word because they want to, not because honesty pays." That article was written in 1990. The world has changed since then. The economy and how we communicate have changed. We are more skeptical now than ever before. Information is more accessible and being an optimist, I believe people choose honesty.

Whether it's good or bad, people always want the truth. It is not just me who thinks this way. In 2014, Edelman asked what specific actions CEOs could take to build trust. Eighty-two per cent gave a top importance rating to "clear and transparent communication," and 81 per cent said it is necessary to tell the truth regardless of how complex or unpopular it is.

SHARE AS MUCH INFORMATION AS YOU CAN

One way to build trust within your organization is to share as much information as you can with your stakeholders. Be as open as you can be, even if the truth is uncomfortable or unfavourable to the organization. When organizations tell the truth, even when it is difficult, barriers are broken down. Trust and transparency allow companies and employees to humanize themselves and earn the respect of customers.

Demonstrating integrity, openness, confidence and honesty is essential to building trustworthy relationships. Leaders and employees in organizations that value honest communications understand they are taking risks and making themselves somewhat vulnerable. They are also being authentic. If a company says, "We do not have the skills in-house to do that project for you, however we know a company that does" this honesty builds credibility and ultimately contributes to building a relationship of trust.

Sometimes honesty is difficult, no doubt. The path of least resistance often seems attractive. Employees might have obligations to themselves, the profession, other colleagues, the company they work for, shareholders, and the customer. They might be wondering, "Is it the right thing to do for the customer to be honest?" "Will I look like I do not know what I am doing?" "Will my company be upset if I tell the customer the truth that the project will not be completed on time?" Customers are people. Most people are understanding when they are being treated fairly. If organizations don't provide the information they need, customers will go looking for the answers on their own.

Everyone appreciates honesty. Honesty leads to stronger relationships. It is a moral choice.

Transparency is a key behaviour that builds trust. When I use the term transparent, I am referring to sharing information that may affect the customer. I am not suggesting that organizations share company competitive information or their commercial secrets. But information that affects the stakeholder should be shared, such as: the hours required to complete a job; the phases in a project; how or where a product is made; why it takes as long as it does to give the customer an answer, to give just a few examples.

Here are some ways to demonstrate transparency:

- Invite customers, distributors and partners to offices, plants, and manufacturing facilities for tours and/or meetings
- Invite customers to question and answer sessions with product management, the engineering team, security or other key service providers
- Post videos that honestly show how your product is made
- Proactively make customers and stakeholders aware of personnel changes
- Invite customers to company events

One simple phrase that encourages sharing of information and promotes trust is the simple but difficult admission "I don't know." Admitting you don't know something doesn't always damage your credibility, unless it is something that has been specifically tasked to know. In fact, "I don't know" can build credibility. No one knows all the answers, if you do not know the answer and you admit that you don't, it shows you are self aware and confident enough to admit it. Depending on the situation, it may demonstrate humility.

If you do not know the answer, be as specific as possible, immediately tell the customer or client something positive, such as " I do not have the information at my finger tips but this is what I can tell you right now." Make sure to offer to get that information as soon as possible.

Examples of honest, transparent and frank speech:

- "This product will not solve your problem or help you achieve your goal."
- "This investment is too risky, you should not buy it."
- "The monthly service fee you are paying is more than you need, we should probably scale it back."
- "We did not pick your shipment up on time."
- "We overcharged you by mistake."
- "We didn't spend as much time on the project as we estimated we would."
- "In my professional opinion, this is not the right thing for you to do."

Ways to introduce doubt and distrust:

1. Exaggerating facts, experience or references

2. Sugar-coating the situation

3. Talking about the competition in an unfavourable light

4. Being afraid to honestly respond to customer's questions and concerns

5. Withholding unpleasant information that the customer should have

6. Reluctance to raise concerns about a client's situation

7. Not admitting the product or service failed some customers

8. Not correcting a misperception the customer has
    (regardless of whether it is good or bad)

9. Withholding info or your professional opinion simply to avoid
    the issue or because the customer might consider it negative
    information or negative news

10. Failing to disclose a conflict of interest

11. Burying information in the 'terms and conditions' or in the
    'fine print' and neglecting to point it out to the customers

12. Breaking another person or organization's confidence by
    speaking about them, such as sharing information that should
    not be shared or gossiping

When someone finds out that information has been hidden from them, they instinctively wonder, "What else are the keeping from us?" This is a sure way to introduce distrust.

DISCLOSING CONFLICTS OF INTEREST

I have a customer, whom I will call Henry. He was a student in my Becoming a Trusted Advisor online course. After the module on honesty and transparency he called me for advice. Henry was feeling uncomfortable about a work situation he was experiencing as the lead account manager for his company's largest customer. The company provides technology solutions to telecommunication and broadband providers. Henry had been working to grow the business and to develop relationships with this customer for two years. He was seeking advice because his employer asked him to go after the business of one of his account's competitors. The competitor called the company for more information. Henry asked me what I thought.

I advised him that it was a perceived or real conflict of interest and suggested he reconsider whether it would be best for him to manage company A's account as well as their competitor's account.

I asked him how he thought his current customer would feel about it. Was this in their best interest or his? I suggested being open and transparent with the customer, to discuss it with his manager and suggest that someone else in the company work with that account. If Henry was uncomfortable, imagine how the customer would feel.

Trusted advisors disclose perceived conflicts of interest.

TAKE THE INITIATIVE - UNCOMFORTABLE TOPICS AND MISCONCEPTIONS

You know that feeling when you sense someone is not telling the truth? I call it 'Spidey senses.' Triggers can be exaggeration, sugar coating, evasion, vagueness or indirect answers. Spidey senses can also be raised when someone is telling the truth but looks dishonest because they are uncomfortable with the topic. Ultimately, when body language is not congruent with the words someone is saying, we know something is wrong. In Amy Cuddy's book, Presence: Bringing Your Boldest Self to Your Biggest Challenges, she explains how to discover if someone is a liar. We can sense lies. When this happens, trust erodes.

Sometimes we are being honest and it looks as if we are lying because we are uncomfortable. You can take the initiative in building comfort and confidence by identifying topics and questions customers might have that will make you uncomfortable. Once you identify them script out your key messages, then practice responding to the questions and topics out loud. Yes, out loud. Everyone is different, what makes one person uncomfortable will be different for the next.

The following are examples of topics that make some of my workshop participants uncomfortable:

+ Price increases or how prices are set
+ Competition
+ Dates for product updates
+ Problems with a project or product
+ Who will be working on the project or the account
+ Missed deadlines
+ Termination, dismissal, resignation of another employee
+ Discontinuation of a product or service
+ Commission, fees, compensation

One of my customers, a financial planner, was terrified he would be asked how much money he made from each sale. He said when he was asked this once by a customer his face got red and he knew he was not being straightforward. He admitted he talked around the issue even when he was telling the truth. We sat together and created a one-page document that he could share with customers when they asked about fees and commissions. It detailed how commissions were set for insurance and mutual fund product sales. Now when customers ask him, he is ready with a specific, direct response and a handout.

In addition to dealing with topics that make you uncomfortable, you can also take the initiative by identifying misconceptions people might have about your products and services and script out responses and key messages for those. For example, product and service limitations or advantages and disadvantages of courses of actions you are recommending.

Three Practical ways to eliminate the element of surprise:

1. Let people know a meeting is planned with people on their team, even if they are not invited

2. Send FYI-only emails to let people know about an event or item in the news that may affect them

3. Offer a heads-up on projects coming down the pipe that might affect a colleague or a customer

We don't like hearing about meetings after the fact. There is an old saying that 'knowledge is power.' There are many ways we can interpret this. One way is that we all want to know what is going on. Most professionals want to be prepared; we do not want to be caught off guard. We all want to be "in the loop."

WHEN EMPLOYEES LEAVE THE ORGANIZATION

Some companies insist on strict confidentiality from employees who elect to leave. Departing employees are often not allowed to tell customers or anyone outside the organization they are leaving. Sometimes companies wait until the last day, or worse, after they are gone, to let people know someone has left or is moving on. In many ways this amplifies the situation. Customers, partners and suppliers do not like this. None of us do. But being transparent about it pays off. Your customers are in business, they know that people come and go.

When I resigned from SolutionInc after working there for many years, I shared my plans with my colleagues, clients and outside partners about a month before my last day. People are naturally curious; they want to know the truth. Lacking that, they will often fill in the blanks on their own. But why not let them know ahead of time? Why not give them the opportunity to ask "Why?" To ask "Where are you going?" and or "What will you be doing?" They also want to know who will look after their business now and how this will affect them. They want to know the company's plan.

HISTORY AND ETHICS

- Truth telling comes from religious traditions including the Christian Ten Commandments and the Buddhist Eightfold Path, where it is described as 'right speech.'

- Philosophers from Aristotle and Thomas Aquinas to those of the modern day have written about truth telling. Virtue ethicists such as Aristotle put truth telling in terms of what a person of good character would do. The challenge with this approach is that a good person may choose to tell the truth or tell a lie to be compassionate or courageous. Both can be seen as virtuous actions.

- Jeremy Bentham, John Stuart Mill, and the other Utilitarians argue there are some conditions where lying is acceptable, if it is done for the greater good. Winston Churchill was quoted warning that "in wartime, truth is so precious that she should always be attended by a bodyguard of lies." Utilitarians place the emphasis on the specific outcome of the ethical decision.

- Duty-based ethicists are more absolute. They argue that even if lying has the better consequence, it is morally wrong to lie. Thomas Aquinas stated that all lies are wrong, but that only some lies are moral sins, while German philosopher Immanuel Kant's categorical imperative states that we are obligated to tell the truth all the time as a sense of duty.

- Rhetoric scholar Dietrich Bonhoeffer wrote, "What is Meant By 'Telling the Truth'?" in Ethics. He argued truth telling is a rich and ethical approach to communication and that is 'intensely situational'. Scholar Ned O'Gorman argues that Bonhoeffer's approach is derived from Aristotle's vision of the good, specifically, the social good.

IMPORTANCE OF TRUTH TELLING

Truth telling is a fundamental ethical issue and constitutes a basic principle and value of many professions including medicine, nursing, engineering and public relations to name a few. Other values of public relations include: veracity (truth-telling), non-maleficence (doing no harm to any parties involved or to society), beneficence (doing good) and fairness (social responsibility).

According to the Canadian Public Relations Society (CPRS) and the Public Relations Society of America (PRSA), telling the truth is an important aspect of practicing ethical public relations. The CPRS code of ethics states that, "A member shall practice the highest standards of honesty, accuracy, integrity and truth, and shall not knowingly disseminate false or misleading information." The PRSA member code of ethics states that practitioners are to "adhere to the highest standards of accuracy and truth in advancing the interests of those [they] represent and in communicating with the public."

Many of my research participants mentioned transparency as a key behaviour.

A few participating organizations including Four Seasons, The Shaw Group, BDC, Acadian Seaplants and Maple Leaf Foods described inviting distributors and customers to offices, plants, and manufacturing facilities, as activities that demonstrate transparency.

Susan Helstab of Four Seasons invited journalists from the Wall Street Journal to the corporate head quarters after the newspaper published incorrect news about the company. Journalists were encouraged to meet and interview Four Seasons employees to learn more about the company.

---

13 practical ways to always be Honest and Transparent

1. Eliminate surprises. Give as much notice as you can

2. Share as much detail and specific information as you can

3. Attempt to answer the who, what, where, when, and why on all issues that affect the other party

4. Share time lines where appropriate

5. Let colleagues, customers and stakeholders know in advance of changes that will affect them including: changes in personnel, product ingredients, pricing, shipping, return, warranty or engagement policies.

6. Do not exaggerate or overstate the benefits of the product,

service, proposed solution or your capabilities

7. Cite limitations of the product or solution you are discussing

8. Point out the pros and cons or the benefits and risks

9. Outline agreements in one or two pages; avoid fine print, cumbersome contracts and legal contracts if possible

10. Practice honesty as a policy

11. Declare a conflict of interest policy

12. Create customer confidentiality agreements

13. Create employee confidentiality agreements

Principle 4

Be Consistent, Predictable and Reliable

When you are reliable, people can count on you. When you are consistent and predictable, your customers know what to expect. These are significant factors in how we decide to trust. Consistent and predictable behaviour communicates reliability, and reduces the customer's sense of risk. This builds confidence and a belief into another person's behavior. Trust, as we've discussed, is faith in the belief in the future actions of a person or company.

When a business is consistent, predictable and reliable, customers will say things like:
• You can always count on them
• You know what you are going to get when you buy from or work with them
• You know you are always going to get your money's worth
• Nobody ever got fired for selecting them
• If you are not satisfied they will fix it right away
• They have never let me down
• There will never be any surprises with these folks

The definition of predictable is being able to foretell or declare something in advance. People don't like surprises. During my research, the participants of the in-depth interviews reported that reliability is the number one characteristic of a trustworthy organization. People want someone to be there when they say they will be; they want to know what they are going to get; they want the support desk to help them when they need it; and they want the project to be completed on the agreed upon time.

Jamie Irving, publisher and owner of Brunswick News explained the significance of consistency and predictability to any business's bottom line: "The news industry is a lot like a restaurant. In a restaurant, every day is like a new product. You can do it right a hundred times and if you miss it once, you have lost the customer's trust. No surprises. You have to offer consistency every day."

The local coffee shop in my neighbourhood does not "get it right" enough. I like that it is local, however, sometimes the coffee is too strong or it's so hot you burn your tongue, or it's lukewarm. It is not reliable and it is not busy.

Starbucks, on the other hand, is consistent, predictable and reliable. No matter where you buy your Starbucks, the taste, quality and packaging of the coffee is the same. Tim Hortons is also consistent, predictable and reliable. In 2015, Tim Hortons was named the "most trusted brand in Canada." We will investigate this further with a look into the iconic Canadian coffee company later in this chapter.

It's important to remember that even in a long-term relationship, we still have to apply the principles of trust. Trust has to be earned every day. We build trust when every interaction is consistent, predictable and reliable. Almost every industry can learn a lesson about these characteristics from the restaurant industry. It is about the quality of the product and service, the physical atmosphere and the front line server. It is also about how they apply the Eight Principles of Trust, in how they communicate, behave and serve the customer.

Here are examples from other industries:

- After 30 years of going to the same hairstylist once a month, you switch hair stylist after two bad sloppy hair cuts

- After 12 years with a web-hosting company, you switch because for two months in a row your website was down

- After going to the same retail store for years because they carry a product you like, you stop going when they stop carrying one of the items you usually buy

- After getting your gas at a station that offers airline miles, you stop getting gas there when they no longer offer points

Additional examples of predictability and reliability:

- After eight years of renewing an annual support contract, one of my clients switched to a new provider because they were no longer "predictable and reliable." My client relayed to me that after three months of having a different person answer the phone each time they called, usually a person who didn't know their system and personnel, and did not have the technical skills to resolve the issues, they could no longer count on them. My customer said, "We need our machines to run. We are paying for support and we expect reliable and predictable service."

- A speaker's bureau I work with hired a professional speaker to present at many of their conferences. After the first conference with this speaker, the bureau received positive reviews and placed him eight times over a 24-month period, making him one of the most popular and profitable speakers they had. However, the ninth time the speaker cancelled the day of the event because he said he wasn't feeling well, disrupting the entire conference program. They bureau never hired him again.

- I went to the same tailor in my neighbourhood for four years. One time I left a suit to be altered and was counting on picking it up the following Tuesday to take on a business trip. When I arrived to pick up the suit, they said, "I didn't get to it yet, come back in a couple of days." I use a new tailor now. Although she is farther away and charges more, she treats customer deadlines as sacred.

A company's behaviour, the quality of it's products and services, consistency in it's communication, and the competence of it's employees, all contribute to building, strengthening and protecting trust.

In my study, all the participants cited reliability as an important behaviour that inspires trust. Practical examples of reliability, consistency and predictability include: hours of operation, meeting deadlines, being on time for meetings, sending documents when you say you will, returning telephone calls or emails promptly, employees providing reliable predictable service, consistently doing the same thing, and receiving the same quality of service each time.

According to Google's 2015 Zero Moment of Truth study, the average buyer engages in more than 10 pieces of content before making a purchasing decision. You may be reading this and thinking, well it is different in different parts of the world... yes there are cross-cultural nuances. For example, the average Asian buyer in Asia engages in 6.3 pieces of data.

Companies must be consistent, predicable in reliable in with every customers interaction from a conversation a sales representative or an accounting clerk, to a LinkedIn experience, a Yelp response to its advertising.

FAMILIARITY

Familiarity makes it possible to entertain reliable expectations and to assess risk. Familiarity is a precondition for trust, as well as distrust. When we have experience with an organization or individual, the risk of potential problems decreases because we know what has happened in the past. If an organization has a reliable background, one may expect similar behaviour going forward. If an individual has worked with another organization or person on a project in the past, they know from repeated interaction how this person will behave on a project team.

People trust people with whom they have a history. Familiarity makes people feel comfortable. We trust what we know and who we know. In situations where there is no history, individuals often make connections via mutual friends or people from a common city, university, or organization. It can also be built with people who share an interest with a specific cause, issue or organization. For example, music, fitness, or Special Olympics.

> Establishing a common ground creates familiarity, which creates a sense of connection and ultimately a sense of trust.

Ways to increase trust when there is no history or familiarity:

- Traditional and social media exposure
- Partnering with an established brand (company or person)
- Aligning the company with others in the industry
- Communicating the strength and experience of employees
- Receiving a reference or referral from another company or trusted industry source

When we conduct the Client Trust Index™ for clients, we often ask their customers the following qualifying questions: How long have you been in this business relationship? How many products or services have you purchased from them? How many projects they have completed? In some cases, the Trust Equity is higher when the relationship is new (less than two years) and/or in cases with only a few projects completed. We will look at this relationship further in chapter 6, Protecting Your Trust Equity.

CONSISTENCY IS NOT A PRIORITY FOR EVERY COMPANY, AND IT AFFECTS THE BOTTOM LINE

I worked with a U.S.-based ICT company whose customers and staff would likely rank this principle area as low. I noticed indicators with this company that their internal culture did not support the ideal of "consistent, predictable and reliable." I say this because from my dealings with them I noticed their follow-up was poor and there was a notable lack of respect for other people's time, expressed through showing up late for meetings. There were even inconsistencies in how email signatures were used. Some had logo and title of their position while others had phone number and name. This variation of the brand and email signature made me wonder if there was a consistent process or policy on how to engage with customers. The vice president of sales and marketing told me they were losing mature customers. Their lack of consistency might have been one reason why.

You may ask, as I have: Doesn't the CEO see this disconnect, inconsistency and lack of reliability? This culture comes from the top and permeates through the organization. As we discussed in Your Hidden Asset chapter, it starts at the top.

MEETINGS AND AGENDAS ARE CONCRETE TOOLS TO BUILD TRUST

A meeting is an important, usually productive, interaction between customer and business. Take them seriously. Avoid cancellations or rescheduling if possible. When you reschedule it makes the customer feel they are not as important. If you make a change to the schedule, plan, agenda or the personnel attending the meeting or working on an account, let the customer know right away. Minimize any and all surprises.

If you must reschedule a meeting, here are three tips to follow:

1. Give ample notice.
2. Let your customer know face to face. If this isn't possible, call, text or snapchat them. Contact them in the way they like to be contacted. Email is passive, and the least personal way of communicating.
3. Explain. Why did you feel it necessary to reschedule?

Trusted advisors set agendas with customers and manage expectations. When you take the customer through a high-level agenda setting discussion, you are setting expectations for what is to come. People like to be prepared. Begin your meeting by asking: "What has changed since we last met? Is there anything we should be aware of?" Next, involve the customer in the agenda setting. Studies show customers involved in decision-making are more engaged and positive about the process. Ask the customer, "What do you want to accomplish?"

Consistency is a critical dimension to setting expectations. We need to know what to expect. We want to know what we are going to get. Trusted advisors provide predictable, reliable results to the customer every time. They treat everyone the same and are the same person at all times.

Three meeting rules to enhance credibility, predictability and reliability

1. Pre-call planning. Preparation is the key to a successful meeting. Have a pre-meeting checklist ready. It should include:

   - An outline of objectives for the call, visit, luncheon, seminar, webinar, dinner, meeting or demonstration
   - Review notes from past calls and meetings, so you are aware of the customer's situation, issues and potential opportunities
   - Have examples ready to show the customer
   - Anticipate customer concerns and objectives

2. Start on time and stick to the schedule. This means be ready 10 minutes before the start time, and end on time.

3. Summarize. At the end the meeting, summarize with conclusions, decisions made and action items. Outline the expectations for the action items and next steps.

TRADITIONS AND CONSISTENCY

There is a lot to be said for consistency. I have been going to one of my former client's charity golf tournaments for many years. The company I worked with, SolutionInc, sponsored a team and the same core group of people played every year. It was a fantastic event that everyone looked forward to.

One year, we could not attend. The tournament dates fell on the same days as a major industry trade show, at which we were committed to speaking and showcasing our product. This was the first time in five years we were not sponsoring and attending the golf tournament. When we let the customer know we wouldn't be going, the customer immediately asked, "What is going on? Is everything okay? What does this mean?" When we explained that we would be away at the trade show, they understood but were still disappointed. The next year, SolutionInc was the first to register to be a sponsor and the company has attended it every year since.

In my research, 100 per cent of participants interviewed cited reliability as the number one characteristic of trustworthy behaviour. In this example, the customer relied on SolutionInc to participate. Any change upsets the proverbial apple cart.

> Traditions and rituals are an effective way to build, strengthen and protect trust.

Doubts can be created if your company participates in an industry event every year and one year decides not to. It is the same with family traditions. For example, if your mother didn't make her sweet potato casserole at Thanksgiving, you might ask, "Mom, what happened? Are you okay? We always have sweet potato casserole at Thanksgiving."

If you have a booth at a trade show a few years in a row, and then you don't the following year, customers may ask "I wonder if they went out of business?" or "I wonder if they have fallen on hard times and can't afford a booth?" or "Perhaps they no longer do business in this industry." Participating in the same event every year builds trust. This consistent, predictable and reliable presence introduces stability.

DEALING WITH CHANGE

Volumes have been written about how to deal with change, change management, and the fact that people do not like change. I actually think people do like change; they just want to be involved. Generally, we do not want change imposed on us, and we do not like surprises. Change raises doubts and fear, which erodes trust.

Here are a few examples of changes and lack of consistency in the workplace that if not communicated properly can introduce distrust:

- Frequent changes in personnel

- Changes to price list, pricing policies, marketing credits or commission

- Warranty and/or support changes

- Product changes

- Licensing changes

- Multiple policy changes over a short period of time

- Saying one thing to one person and something else to another

- Participation at events

- Process of procedural changes

- Deadline, shipping or project timeline changes

Ten practical tips to apply for consistency, predictability and reliability in your organization

1. Consistent messages engender trust. Say the same things over and over. Inconsistent messages or different messages from different people create mistrust. Inconsistencies suggest you can't trust what someone says. This is one reason why it is best practice for companies to have a spokesperson, or communication/public relations professional publish the key messages. When one person is communicating a message there is a greater chance of accuracy and less chance of inconsistency.

2. Provide regular updates. When we are working on a project with a customer, we give them a daily or end-of-week update. Last year my husband and I worked with a Royal LePage Atlantic real estate agent to sell our cottage. Every Friday, the agent contacted us with a weekly update. Sometimes he said there was nothing new, but we knew that on Friday he was thinking about our property and about us. And we appreciated that we didn't have to call him to find out how things were going.

3. Set and manage expectations. This is a key skill that every trusted advisor and professional should master. Decide what you're going to do, communicate it and then do it.

4. Ensure your approach and tone are consistent with a customer-focused approach. For example, if you have an issue with Amazon, which is widely known for the excellence in customer service, you get the same tone of response, answer, and approach from anyone you interact with, whether it's online or over the phone.

5. Outline the professional code of conduct: I have an accounting firm as a client that that has clearly outlined its professional code of conduct for its employees and customers. They state they will return calls and emails within a specific time and update customers at regular intervals for long-running projects. They even send emails to acknowledge holiday greeting cards! Their commitment to accountability and building relationships of trust differentiates them in the marketplace. Because of this, the company has grown quickly in its first three years of business.

6. Follow up - return phone calls. Following up with people is extremely important. We always remember when someone fails to call us back. Sometimes it is embedded in our memory that someone did not follow up when they said they would. When someone responds, it signals to us that we are important. When people fail to follow-up, it says we are not important.

   Every time I mention the name of a particular public affairs firm to my father, he says things like, "That managing partner is not reliable. He doesn't return phone calls. I would never deal with them again. They are not reliable and they are disrespectful." This happened in 1999. Almost 20 years ago. My father has told dozens of people about this man and he openly tells people that the firm is not reliable. Returning phone calls, texts, and responding to emails is important. As we have already discussed, 96 per cent of people never complain. Of them, 91 per cent just leave and never come back.

7. Distribute company policies, procedures and guidelines including pricing, social media use and partnership policies.

8. Attach performance measurements and compensate employees for executing and performing to the correct standards.

9. Allow plenty of lead time to inform people of changes to policies, procedures and personnel.

10. Inform and notify people of changes multiple times in writing and verbally. I would recommend at least five times.

The little things count. It is easier to do business with people who are consistent.

TIM HORTONS: ONE OF THE MOST TRUSTED BRANDS IN CANADA

In 2015, Tim Hortons was named the most trusted brand in Canada according to the Gustavson Brand Index.

From the outside looking in, as a customer, shareholder and former employee (in the 1980s serving coffee and donuts), Tims Hortons clearly practices the Eight Principles of Building and Protecting Trust.

Here are a just some examples of how Tim Hortons has built a trusted brand with Canadians.

+   Tim Hortons is *predictable, consistent and reliable*. This is one of their greatest strengths. Research shows that reliability is the number one criteria to build trust. We know what to expect and there is consistency in everything we see and experience including their products, policies, locations, and messages. The coffee is always hot, the products taste the same in every store, and the locations all look similar. Predictability, consistency and reliability reduce vulnerability and risk. When risk decreases, trust can increase.

+ Tim Hortons delivers on its promise of 'always fresh'. The coffee is always fresh, wherever you are — whether you're in Whitehorse, Calgary, Toronto, Fredericton, or St. John's. The polices and practices are aligned with the company promise.

+ Tim Hortons demonstrates that they are listening to their customers by continuing to improve and innovate their products and their stores. They replaced the individual tea bag with fresh brewed tea years ago in response to customer requests. More recently, they added dark roast coffee to appeal to the tastes of their customers after receiving feedback in 2013 that's what people wanted.

+ Tim Hortons stores demonstrate *transparency* with glass and open kitchen areas and nutrition information. For example, they openly report that the strawberry filled donut has 31 g of sugar and 290 calories. Most locations make the sandwiches in front of us so we can see the ingredients. In many locations ovens are out front and in some of the newly designed stores you can watch them coat and dip donuts in sugar glaze from the counter.

+ Across Canada, Tim Hortons demonstrates its commitment to the communities where they operate. They sponsor events such as youth sports and the Tim Horton Children's Foundation. Being a socially responsible corporate citizen strengthens a company's reputation for trustworthiness.

+ Lastly, Tim Hortons shows us that they are committed to the long term of building and strengthening the trust by surveying its customers regularly.

These are just some examples of how Tim Hortons has become the most trusted brand in Canada. Tim Hortons' consistency demonstrates trust and inspires: commitment, confidence, credibility, familiarity, stability and predictability.

Consider the following when evaluating your organization's consistency:

- ✓ Logo: appearance and use of

- ✓ Email signatures and email syntax

- ✓ Employee's LinkedIn photos

- ✓ How people answer the phone

- ✓ Voicemails

- ✓ Invoicing

- ✓ Shipping

- ✓ Packaging

- ✓ Proposals

- ✓ Lead time for orders

- ✓ Signage

- ✓ Ability to track orders

- ✓ Interactions with technical staff

- ✓ Company name

- ✓ Hours of operation

QUESTIONS TO ASK ABOUT YOUR ORGANIZATION WHEN YOU ARE EVALUATING ITS CONSISTENCY, PREDICTABILITY AND RELIABILITY

1. Are you providing services that customers expect?

2. Do you meet deadlines?

3. Does everyone in the company deliver the same quality of service?

4. Does everyone describe the products, services, policies or procedures, etc. the same way?

5. Would your stakeholders think you are predictable?

6. Does every employee get treated the same way?

7. Does every office or every location look the same?

8. How often do the policies or procedures change?

9. Is the look of the website consistent with the look of your proposals?

10. Do the employees all treat the customers and the suppliers the same way?

Consistent and predictable behaviour communicates reliability and reduces the customer's sense of risk.

Principle 5

Act in the Best Interests of Customers, Stakeholders and the Public

Intentions and motives are key to building, strengthening and protecting relationships. Your customer or stakeholder must believe that you and your organization are putting their interests first. Trust development will only succeed when expectations are met and motives are clear.

Several summers ago we took a family holiday trip to Maine. We were driving from Halifax to Portland, an eight or nine hour drive. An hour in, we noticed the car was making a loud noise. My husband figured it needed a new muffler. When we got to Portland we went to a drive-through service station, but if you've ever been to Maine in August you'll know it's an extremely busy place. You're lucky to get a seat in a restaurant, let alone a drive-through mechanic. It would take days before we could see a mechanic. The car continued to make the sound, but we kept driving. We had a lovely holiday and made it back safe and sound. The day after we got home I took the car to a place to have the muffler fixed. I left the keys with the man at the front desk with my phone number and told him I'd be back at the end of the day to pick it up.

About 20 minutes later, my phone rang, "This is Glen from Speedy Muffler and I have some good news and bad news." I said to tell me the bad news first. He said, "It's not the muffler. You need an entirely new exhaust system. We don't have the parts you need." My heart sank, I was thinking about all the money we'd just spent on our vacation, and said, "Ok, what's the good news?" He said, "The good news is that I checked the mileage on your car and the exhaust system is still under warranty. You have 2,000 km left on your warranty. I called the dealership for you. They are expecting your car and they can fix it this week. Just don't make any big trips."

Glen at Speedy Muffler acted in my best interest. When I went in to his shop that Monday morning, he was there along with three other mechanics. They have four bays and I was the only one there. He gave up a sale to do the right thing for me, his customer. Now, my husband and I both get our cars serviced at Glen's Speedy Muffler in Halifax. They look after our tires, oil changes and brakes. I trust Glen because he acts in our best interest.

When I tell this story to customers I ask if they have a mechanic they can trust, they often say no. They tell me stories of mechanics telling them they need brake pads when they don't, or that their tires will perform better if they're on rims, or that it's going to take an hour to put on new windshield wipers. When we hear these things, we wonder if they get a commission or bonus to sell us something. For those of us who don't know anything about cars and just want theirs to run smoothly, we need a mechanic we can trust.

This principle is often the most difficult for companies and organizations. When we conduct the Client Trust Index™ for clients, their customers usually rate this Principle the lowest. Even clients that have a strong trust with their customers tend to score lower. The figure below shows actual ratings customers gave one of my clients.

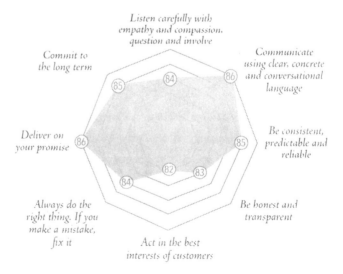

Many companies often have a difficult time getting their heads around putting the public's or their customer's interest ahead of their own. But when they do, they have loyal customers.

Recently, on a summer Friday afternoon, I called my accountant to ask a few tax questions. To my frustration, I was told she just left for holiday and would be away for two weeks. Before I could say anything, the person that answered the phone asked, "Is there anything I can help you with?" Reluctantly, I explained what I was looking for. To my complete satisfaction, he answered all my questions. There was no checking with management, no red tape. This is an example of how a company can demonstrate that employees are putting their customers interests first, regardless of their job description. The man I spoke to was a junior bookkeeper who knew nothing about my business, but he took the time to help me navigate through my questions and locate the information I was looking for.

> About 70 per cent of buying experiences are based on how the customer feels they are being treated, according to McKinsey & Company. We want to buy from companies we feel good about, companies that we trust to put our interests first. Since every employee has a role to play in the customer's decision to do business with your company, it makes sense that instilling a customer centred trust culture to grow your business is the top priority for many successful companies.

WHERE DO YOUR LOYALTIES LIE?

One of the reasons people might find it hard to act in the customer's best interest and not their own, is because they have competing loyalties. If you really want to be trusted, you need to put the person you are dealing with first, you need to be honest with them and share your intentions.

For example, if a U.S. customer asked a survey company to do an analysis of them in November, and the survey company said "Sure." I might ask, "Are they really acting in the customer's best interest here?" I say this because the U.S. Thanksgiving holiday is the third week of November. Most offices close down, not a lot of business happens on Thanksgiving Day, and four weeks later Christmas arrives. Depending on the year, Hanukkah and Ramadan might also fall within that four-week period. Shortly after that is Chinese New Year.

Based on the holidays it may not be in the customer's best interest to conduct a survey between November 15 and the middle of January as the company may not get the best response rate. A survey company that is acting in their own best interest might push ahead because they want the work. If the situation of unreliably data is explained to the customer, and the company still says they want it done, then you are in the clear to go ahead, as you've notified them of your opinion.

To summarize, don't try to sell the customer something that is not right for them.

As I have mentioned, I sometimes ask seminar participants to give examples of companies they trust. They often name companies such as L.L. Bean, Wal-Mart and Costco. When I ask them why, they say one of the best things about these companies is that they know they can "take stuff back," "they make it easy for customers," "their return policies are focused on the customer's interests," and "they stand behind their return policies."

L.L. BEAN CUSTOMER CENTRED TRUST STRENGTHENING POLICIES

L.L. Bean is an outdoor equipment retail store that started in Freeport, Maine more than 100 years ago. They have a customer return policy that states they want their customers to be 100 per cent satisfied. This policy is clearly identified on their website, all receipts, and even on their gift cards. For them, it's about acting in the customer's best interest. Ultimately, they want their customers to be loyal.

Several years ago, while on vacation with my family in Maine, we took an L.L. Bean kayaking adventure camp. It was a one-day camp. Everyone meets at the store, and then you get on the green L.L. Bean bus and they take you to an inlet on the coast. There, you learn how to kayak using their equipment. At the end of this camp, someone complained and said they didn't have fun and wanted their money back. I was surprised. The weather was warm and the water was calm. It was a perfect day and a perfect camp. We were in the middle of the woods on the way back to the bus, and I watched the instructor give this customer a gift certificate for the amount of the camp. I'd always heard of great customer service, and I was witnessing it here for myself. When I got back to the store I talked to the employee who gave out the gift certificate. I asked him to tell me about their policy. He said, "It's very simple. We want all of our customers to be happy. We want all our customers to be 100 per cent satisfied with the quality of our products and services. If they're not, we will do whatever we can to make it right for them."

I asked him how this affects their sales numbers. He said, "Every year returns and refunds are a percentage of our bottom line, however, it's more important to us that customers are happy. We know that if we always act in our customer's best interest, and go with our philosophy, they will reward us, and they have." A colleague told me he heard a podcast in which L.L. Bean explained its policy. "People were returning boots they had for 10 years and they were replaced, no questions asked." He found it "quite amazing."

> It takes a lot longer and is far more expensive to get a new cus-
> tomer than to maintain a good relationship with an existing one.

You may be thinking your company has a different business model and is not set up to do this. I work with all types of businesses, and the same rules always apply. With an accounting firm, as an example, their model is to charge the customer for their time. They will do your taxes and charge you for the amount of time it takes. If you ask an accounting firm for advice, they could charge you for every minute they are thinking about you, discussing your file, preparing recommendations and sharing the information.

Some people might think charging for every minute is not acting the customer's best interest. Many of us want to deal with professionals who are trusted advisors, but the kind of trusted advisors who do not bill by the minute. One of my clients, an accounting firm, has tweaked their business model because they want to have outstanding relationships with their customers. They want to have exceptional trust equity with their clients.

The following are a few practical ways an accounting firm, or a firm with a similar business model, could demonstrate they working to act in their customer's best interests:

1. Share with the customer how they can reduce their bill. For example, if you're an accounting firm you can suggest your customer have all their receipts in order as opposed to a shoebox of receipts.

2. Share new laws with customers so they are up to date. For example, if a new income tax law changes the taxable percentages in your region, proactively share this with customers.

3. Share customer information with preparers, junior accountants and entry-level professionals so they understand what they're working on, why it's important to the customer, and how their work affects them.

WORKING ON COMMISSION

A commissioned sales person makes money by selling you something; therefore, they are financially motivated to sell. And the reality is, none of us want to be sold to. Many organizations do not have sales associates 'on commission' for this very reason.

The car industry is famous for commission sales and we all know when you work in a car dealership that's how you get paid. It's probably not a coincidence that car salespeople are among the least trusted occupations. This is a blanket statement, however, it is also backed up by polls.

In addition to car salespeople, other professions that are considered untrustworthy are insurance and advertising sales representatives, and stockbrokers. These occupations all have commission in common. Sometimes, commission drives people and they think only about themselves. They are not recommending products, services or offerings that are in the customer's best interest.

You know you've found a salesperson that is acting in your best interest when they tell you, "This is not the right product for you" or "You might want to try Company ABC" or "Company X has a better product for your needs." Or they say, "Here's a way you can get this solution within your budget and save money."

For example, if you live in northern Ontario a car salesperson might suggest you don't need air conditioning as a way to get your payments lower. If you're a stockbroker you might remind your customer that every single trade is costing them money and suggest they be put on a different payment structure. A trusted insurance advisor lets customers know that if they choose one type of policy over another, they can save money long-term on fees.

MOTIVES, INTENTIONS AND MUTUAL UNDERSTANDING

Trust benefits from mutual understanding and intimacy. If you are close with the person with whom you are building trust, you have a better chance to achieve exceptional trust. For example, if a company plans to change its service policy and shares the reason for the change in policy with customers, it will have a greater likelihood of gaining and protecting the customer's trust.

Openly communicating motives in a timely fashion builds trust. In a 'timely fashion' is key. No one likes surprises. When making a policy change, make sure you give your customers ample notification of the policy, procedural, personnel and/or schedule changes that may affect them.

> Mutual awareness is key to holding relationships of trust together.

Your customers and stakeholders are wondering what your motives and intentions are. In fact, they are deciding to trust based on your organization's past practices and future plans. Acting in the their best interests is a way you can demonstrate your motives are sincere, authentic and with them foremost in mind.

BIRD CONSTRUCTION: A TRUST LEADER ACTING IN THE BEST INTERESTS OF ITS CLIENTS AND COMMUNITY

In May 2016, a devastating forest fire swept through Fort McMurray, Alberta, and burned down much of the city. Fort McMurray has a population of 61,000 and is a bustling North American oil hub. The fire left devastation and destroyed families, homes, businesses and schools. Bird Construction was awarded the contract to rebuild a school in Fort McMurray. Bird Construction is one of Canada's leading construction companies and general contractors, with offices and projects across Canada.

Without payment, Bird Construction started the project to rebuild a school for the community. When the insurance company pays the claim, their customer will be able to pay for the construction. Without Bird Construction, students would not have a school. This is not a well-known fact. A project manager at Bird Construction shared this story with me six months after the fire and months after the project had started. At that time, the insurance company still hadn't settled or paid the claim to rebuild the school. This example of acting in the customer's best interest and doing the right thing for the community demonstrates Bird Construction's integrity. It shows their compassion and intent to do the right thing for their customer, the students and the community.

In his book, Managing in the Gray: Five Timeless Questions for Resolving Your Toughest Problems at Work, Harvard ethics professor Joseph L. Badaracco suggests five basic questions for leaders to ask when making decisions in situations where the data and facts are not clear. He suggests the questions can also help you when you are wondering if you are acting in the customer's best interests, and when you are deciding whether or not you are doing the right thing.

The questions are:

1. What are the net consequences? Consider the consequences for everyone who is going to be affected.
2. What are my core obligations? Consequences are important, but so are core human obligations, and there are some things that are just wrong and you can't do them.
3. What will work in the world as it is?
4. Who are we? He discusses testing decisions against core values, what the organization cares about and how it treats people.
5. What can I live with?

EVALUATE YOUR ORGANIZATION.
ARE YOU GIVING THE CUSTOMER'S BEST INTERESTS THE HIGHEST PRIORITY?

1. Do we truly understand our customers? Holistically?

2. Are employees empowered to act in the best interests of the customer even if it might cost the company money?

3. Do we offer customers advice on the price and service options available to them? Do we recommend other reputable companies if they can better meet the customer's needs? Do we inform customers when we do not have the skills required to do the work? Do we recommend they hire another company?

4. Do your employees help customers be better advocates for themselves by encouraging them to always read the fine print?

5. Do we offer financial incentives to employees to sell customers things they do not need, or want?

6. Does everyone understand the impact their work is making on the customers?

Note: Depending on your organization's purpose and what it does, the principle might be adapted from acting in the customer's best interest to: acting in the industry's best interest or the profession's, member's, volunteer's, the community, etc.

Principle 6

Do the Right Thing.
If You Make a Mistake, Fix It.

More than 100 years ago, French sociologist Emile Durkheim proposed that there are several areas of unspoken, taken-for-granted agreements in societies that constitute a "concscience collectif." Translated, this means "collective consciousness." Trust is most often unspoken. It is an agreement among individuals that is taken for granted until it is betrayed.

In January 2017, Edelman reported that only 52 per cent of people said they trust businesses to do what is right. When we consider this statistic, we are forced to ask ourselves, "Is trust still part of the concscience collectif?"

Doing the right thing is an expression of your values, integrity and ethics. Ethics becomes part of the fabric of a trusted organization's culture. Many of the executives I have interviewed said doing what is right is one of their core values. For example, when I interviewed Susan Helstab, executive vice president of the Four Seasons about the company's culture, she said, "Trust is so implicit, it doesn't need to be said. It is foundational to our culture of following the golden rule of treating others as we would like to be treated."

Because companies are made up of people, and none of us is perfect, all companies make mistakes. When we make a mistake, we want someone to fix it so we're happy with the outcome and we have a good experience. Oftentimes, it's about how the company fixes it and the experience we have during that process that builds trust. In fact, sometimes we have more trust in a company after they've made a mistake because they've fixed it and acknowledged the mistake in a way that built trust.

Showing commitment to fixing a mistake, if you make one, builds trust. It is often said that how a company deals with a situation, complaint or a mistake will actually develop more trust with customers and partners. Put another way, mistakes can be seen as opportunities. There are critical trust risk points for organizations — significant events in the customer or stakeholder's experience with the organization that can build, strengthen or destroy trust. Often, these experiences carry an emotional element, which heightens the sensation, good or bad. It is during these times that organizations, large and small, can demonstrate how trustworthy they are. We discussed this in Principle 5 when we looked at Costco and L.L. Bean.

Top Talent Connector Chris Henry says, "I trust companies that do the right thing. When I am looking to connect top talent, I look at companies and consider if they have a high Client Trust Index™ score."

Having spent the majority of his career in IT, five years as the CIO for Grant Thornton in Canada and 16 years at Four Seasons Hotels and Resorts in various IT roles including corporate director of IT operations, Chris knows the importance of fixing mistakes, in fact he tells people "Don't forget to DUCK when approached with a glitch." As he says, "When there is a glitch you need to resolve it." Chris suggests doing this by DUCKing — which stands for Diffuse [the situation] Understand [the situation] Collaborate [and treat with] Kindness."

> Diffuse [the situation] Understand [the situation] Collaborate [and treat with] Kindness - Chris Henry

A recent study revealed that people trust local, family-run businesses more than big corporations. According to Edelman, 80 per cent of people trust family-owned businesses. However, family-owned businesses often make the same mistakes as multi-billion dollar, publically traded companies.

About five years ago we renovated our kitchen. As part of the renovation, we changed the flooring from vinyl to tile. My husband and I worked with an interior designer who recommended a local, family-owned flooring company to help us choose new tile. The company was great and the floor turned out beautiful. However, after about a month, the grout between a few of the tiles started cracking.

We called the tile company as soon as we noticed it. Their phone system is automated and I couldn't get a person on the phone. When I finally spoke to someone I asked to leave a message for the manager. No one got back to me. After six months, a few tiles started to crack. I left more messages, but the company was ignoring my calls. I suspect that in their eyes, the job was finished. We paid the bill and it was clear they were not planning to honour the 25-year warranty.

After being a customer of our local dance school for seven years, my daughter decided halfway through the year she didn't want to continue. I pulled out the policy to review the cancellation policy. The policy stated 30 days notice needed to be given. So on January 12, I called and wrote an email that we would be stopping classes on February 12. At that time, I asked for them to stop the automatic credit card payments. They agreed.

But on February 1 they informed me that even though the written policy was 30 days, since I paid monthly, I would have to pay an extra month. This was apparently an unwritten rule. This was not written anywhere — not on the registration contract I signed, nor was it on the website or the credit card authorization. When I brought this to their attention, they argued with me.

In both cases I did what 58 per cent of the population does, according to the 2011 Edelman Trust Barometer: I told a friend. Actually, I told a few friends. One friend said, "lots of the other parents talk about how often their credit cards are over charged on the monthly fees." I then started doubting how the monthly fees were charged. I learned several others had tiles that cracked from the local flooring company. Having people talk like this about your company is not good for business.

DO NOT ARGUE WITH THE CUSTOMER

Some people believe that to defeat an opponent, aggressive discourse is good. However, when we are conversing to do the right thing and to build trust, the Socratic dialogue of seeking to understand first is typically a faster way to win someone over. As a rule, I would suggest "never argue with the customer." A customer's interests must always be at the forefront. This doesn't mean the customer is always right.

According to Winston Churchill, every question can be given a response that is clear, concise, perfectly logical and dead wrong. So just because you can win an argument doesn't mean you should try to. The point behind the expression "The customer is always right," is that even when he or she isn't right, you must respond to their complaint or concern in a positive way for them.

We learn from mistakes. In a culture of trust, mistakes are made, we learn from them and get better as a result. Looking at all the trust leaders I have interviewed during my research, I would suggest all the great leaders have one thing in common: they all say they make mistakes and are not afraid to be vulnerable. They are not too important or too perfect to make mistakes. And they are willing to share what they learned, how they learned it, the mistakes, blunders and the screw-ups they made along the way. They are sincere, genuine and authentic. They relate themselves as a whole person. Great leaders show vulnerability and show they care. They say "I'm sorry" in a meaningful way.

As we will see in the Maple Leaf Foods case study following this chapter, CEO Michael McCain demonstrated vulnerability during a crisis for the company. He was sincere, authentic and vulnerable in his apology.

Great leaders show vulnerability and show they care.

APOLOGIES: THE GOOD AND THE BAD

Good apologies accept full responsibility, communicate sincerity and acknowledge the person or people affected. Great ones are courageous and show vulnerability.

Checklist for apologies:
- Timely
- Sincere
- Empathetic
- Compassionate
- Accountable
- Courageous
- Show vulnerability

Bad apologies in many cases can be worse than no apology at all. Bad apologies destroy trust. They typically do not address the issue instead they blame someone or something else, ask for sympathy, are insincere, and take place too long after the event.

ETHICS AND TRUST

Ethics is a topic that permeates all aspects of our lives. It also has many close ties with trust. Ethics is more than just acting in the customer, public or stakeholder's best interests; it's more than just doing the right thing.

When I taught ethics to fourth-year communications undergraduate students at Mount Saint Vincent University, I would remind students everything they did was a reflection of their values, their morals and their ethics. We would have great discussions about "the prickly side of ethics," and as it was often pointed out, it sometimes does not pay to be ethical.

One must always evaluate the consequences. I know this from my own personal experience. I once confronted a colleague with the truth about a situation. I value honesty, holding confidences and believed I was acting ethically, however, I did not properly evaluate the long-range indirect consequences and I lost a very dear friend.

In business, we are constantly making ethical choices whether we realize it or not. Professionals are constantly balancing an organization's interests against the customer's interests.

Our ethics are rooted in philosophy. The following are a few common philosophical views that have shaped business and professional ethics. They are interesting to consider when you are deciding how you and your organization can act in the best interests of your customers, stakeholders, colleagues and employees and how to do the right thing.

+ The Golden Rule. Virtually every single one of the world's traditions has highlighted and/or mentioned what has become known as the Golden Rule. The most familiar version is, "Do unto others as you would have them do unto you."

+ According to a Chinese sage, we must have "jian ai," which means concern for everybody.

+ Buddha's Golden Rule is a person who loves the self should not harm the self of others.

+ The Socratic method is about asking questions: seeking first to understand, then to be understood. Socrates believed "the unexamined life is not worth living."

- According to Aristotle, moral behaviour is the mean between two extremes - at one end is excess, at the other deficiency. Find a moderate position between those two extremes and you will be acting morally.

- Immanuel Kant's categorical imperative says that sometimes the morally right action may not bring us the best consequences. I once had a customer break a confidence by sharing proprietary information. I confronted the person and we did not move forward with the project as a result of it.

DOING THE RIGHT THING IS CONTAGIOUS

As we have discussed, creating a culture of trust starts at the top with the leadership team and cascades through the entire organization.

Authors of Connected: The Surprising Power of Our Social Networks, and How They Shape our Lives, Dr. Nicholas Christakis and Dr. James Fowler studied various communities in Massachusetts and found that among adults, everything is contagious. For example, if your neighbour goes on a diet, you and your other neighbours are likely to go on diets too. Anger spreads to your family and through social networks.

Their findings also showed that positive emotions and pro-social emotions are more contagious than any others. They spread more rapidly and collectively than the negative.

We know that giving and sharing feels good. There are studies showing that if I share resources with you, I get a little activation in the reward circuit in my brain. There is evidence that these good feelings promote bonding through social networks, even bridging social divisions.

This research is directly related to building trust. Relationships of trust are built on social bonds. Trust with customers and stakeholders is also about social bonds.

When you do the right thing, everyone in the organization feels good. Living by the same values, acting in the customer's best interests and applying the principles of trust, can be contagious.

Everyone on your team can take part in doing the right thing. Every employee can point out and fix mistakes and errors in a timely fashion, listen and respond to complaints, protect privacy, demonstrate ethical behaviour and empower others to do the right thing.

CRITICAL TRUST RISK POINTS

Every organization has critical trust risk points, events when the customer experiences an organization's abilities. Examples would include when a final report is delivered, during the sales process, a safety incident, the delivery of a product, or how a missed deadline is handled. It's at these points where trust is critical because this is when a customer really experiences your organization. This is when they see how you handle things. Sometimes we refer to these times as 'moments of truth'.

In the banking industry, a mortgage renewal can be a critical trust point. For a pipeline, a critical trust point could be the installation of new pipe in an environmental way. If you're an accounting firm, it could be the final signoff of financial statements. If you're a litigator, it's how you do in the courtroom.

In the Acting in the Customer's Best Interest Principle, we discussed companies that people have told me they trust — companies that allow us to return products and services. Similarly to returning, when a company makes a mistake, if we right that wrong in a way that the customer (you!) would be proud of, you build trust. It's about communicating and managing expectations well.

There are lots of examples of companies that have made mistakes and didn't fix them well. There are also a few examples of companies that made mistakes and did a pretty good job fixing them.

JOHNSON AND JOHNSON: CLASSIC EXAMPLE OF CRISIS MANAGEMENT

Johnson and Johnson is a classic example and one of the best. It has been written about for decades. The safety of its product, Tylenol, is a critical trust risk point for Johnson and Johnson. We will discuss critical trust risk points in more detail in Chapter 9.

In 1982, a person or persons unknown tampered with Tylenol in stores in the Chicago area. Cyanide was added to the drug and six people died. It was a terrible tragedy but Johnson and Johnson's handling of it is a textbook example of crisis management. Customers wanted assurances that the product would be safe. In the end, they didn't come right out and say it was a supplier or that it happened in a drug store. They just took ownership and were accountable.

According to a Richard Ruch and Ronald Goodman, authors of Image at the Top: Crisis and Renaissance in Corporate Leadership. James E. Burke, chairman and chief executive officer of Johnson and Johnson said, "One of our greatest strengths as a company is that we have a set of truths in our credo that helps bring us together, even though we are a big company operating worldwide."

The packaging was changed to make it tamper-proof. Customers could easily see whether the Tylenol package they had just bought was free from interference. Within a year, Tylenol regained its market share and Johnson and Johnson is recognized as one of the world's most trusted brands.

ACCOUNTABILITY IS TAKING RESPONSIBILITY

British Petroleum (BP) is an example of a company that did not respond quickly and did not do the right thing.

On April 20, 2010, the Deepwater Horizon semi-submersible oil rig exploded and sank in the Gulf of Mexico, setting off one of the worst oil spills in U.S. history. Eleven people were killed and an estimated 3.19 million barrels of oil leaked into the ocean, causing substantial economic and environmental damage to the states on the Gulf Coast. It took 87 days until the blown-out well was capped and the oil stopped leaking, and many believe the Gulf is still not oil-free to this day. BP received strong public criticism for its role in the disaster and although attention initially focused on the deaths of the 11 employees, it soon shifted to the severe economic losses and environmental destruction from the huge volumes of oil re-leased into the Gulf. Although the total damages to BP, the environment, and the U.S. Gulf Coast economy are estimated to be $36.9 billion, the damage to BP's brand, reputation and trust levels still linger because of how poorly the situation was handled. The CEO was fired, needless to say.

Reputation is based on past experiences. It's based on a perception we have. Trust is based on potential future experiences. It's about the cumulative experiences we have, but it's also a faith and belief that the company is going to act in our best interest, do the right thing and if it makes a mistake it will get fixed. One of the reasons companies can come back from mistakes, as Johnson and Johnson did, is because the error was acknowledged and fixed, the company apologized and did all the right things.

Examples of doing the right thing:

- Honouring a warranty, service or return policy

- Following a code of conduct, or code of ethics

- Apologizing when you do not meet commitments

- Holding employees and colleagues accountable for acting in accordance with the organization's values, mission and purpose

- Focusing on building empathy and compassion with customers and stakeholders

- Protecting the privacy of your employees, suppliers and customers

- Acknowledging and abiding by confidentiality agreements

- Admitting when you do not have the answer, or if your product or service is not the right solution to solve the problem

- Acting on feedback you receive from employees, customers and or stakeholders

Principle 7

Deliver on Your Promise

When we form a new business relationship with someone, we subconsciously evaluate, question and wonder. Are they who they seem to be? What is their track record? Do they do what they say they will do, and what they are supposed to do? Do they have the capabilities to do what they say? Do they consistently perform? What is it like to deal with them? Do they keep their products and services up to date? Will we consistently get the experience we expect? Did they act in the way we expected?

One of my customers is constantly saying he wishes his suppliers would fulfill their promises. This customer does business in the U.S. and Caribbean and his organization depends on suppliers. He asked to remain anonymous. The suppliers include some of North America's largest and most well known companies in the cable, telecommunications, professional services, media and ICT computer industries.

He said to me, "If their service would improve, we would do so much more business with them." I asked him if he trusted his suppliers? Without hesitation, he said, "No. Not many of them. Most of them disappoint. They don't do what they say they are going to do and we can't rely on them."

Here are the top three things suppliers do that bother him the most:

1. **Missed deadlines:** When things are late or don't arrive when expected.

2. **Not thinking about what is best for the customer.** He recounted a story of a supplier knowingly not adjusting to the most efficient shipping mode, even

though they had agreed on a delivery date. "If the supplier paid attention to what was important to us, they would choose a shipment method other than ground so we could receive the product on time and meet our deadline. Instead of thinking about what is important to us, this supplier followed the original rule blindly and shipped via ground." "They take the order, hand it to a guy in shipping and forget about you. No follow up. No instructions. No thought." This type of situation makes it very clear that the supplier does not care enough about them.

3. **Misrepresenting the product.** Companies that claim their product does more than it does will lose credibility and trust with their customers.

As we have discussed, suppliers who build relationships and earn the trust of their customers can become trusted advisors. Trusted advisors consistently deliver on their promises. Promises are part of the core definition of trust.

According to the dictionary, the definition of promise is a declaration that one will do or refrain from doing something specified. Synonyms include covenant, pledge, to swear, vow or to give one's word.

ALL CUSTOMERS WANT WHAT YOUR ORGANIZATION PROMISES TO DELIVER

Employees want to deliver on the promises they make and doing that affects their performance in a positive way. In the book The Progress Principle: Using Small Wins to Ignite Joy, Engagement, and Creativity at Work, authors Teresa Amabile and Steven Kramer find employees deliver when they make progress, even small wins, on work they find meaningful. This finding has significant implications for creating a culture of trust. When company and employee objectives are aligned with the company purpose and vision, and these objectives are being achieved, the company is delivering on its promise. When you deliver on your promise, customers reward you. I repeat: Customers want what your organization promises to deliver.

Organizations demonstrate integrity and build trust by delivering on their promises, keeping commitments, behaving congruently with their values, doing what they say they are going to do, and honouring their word. This principle is about serving, anticipating, meeting and exceeding expectations. When organizations do not follow through with their promises they are perceived to lack integrity.

Integrity is a chief behaviour that leads to trust. For example, if you say you will always have the lowest prices in town, then you should have the lowest prices. If you say you have the best curriculum in your field, then it better be the best. What is your organization's promise? Is it highest quality, outstanding service, best user experience, friendly experts, thorough advice or something unique to your situation?

Marketers may refer to the "brand promise." They will promise "the brand experience." Think of the world's top brands. They deliver on their promises. Let's look at Nike, for example. Nike's promise is: Just do it. For over 50 years Nike has been delivering on that promise.

Mercedes Benz promises "The best or nothing." The company refers specifically to innovation on its website: "We never stop inventing new ways to realize the potential of the road ahead." I have a friend who has driven Mercedes cars for 15 years. He says he buys Mercedes because he trusts the brand and every aspect of the process. "They are thinking about my needs. I drive a lot and they asked me if I'm interested in diesel. I have had the same sales person for 15 years. They put out a high quality product. When my lease is up, I don't even think about another brand."

Four Seasons Hotels and Resorts employees are empowered to wow guests. The hotel promises extraordinary experiences, and continually updates its products and services to do just that. Not only does Four Seasons provide extraordinary experiences at its hotels and resorts, it also offers private jet travel, culinary "wows" and adventures for their guests all around the world. Susan Helstab, former Four Seasons Hotels and Resorts executive vice-president of marketing said the company was "fanatical about delivering on our promise."

Significant elements of delivering on your promise include:

- Execution and follow-up
- Tracking and measuring performance
- Innovation
- Anticipating and meeting expectations

EXECUTION AND FOLLOW-UP

According to Jeffrey Pfeffer of Stanford Business School, there are experts in everything except how to get things done. The March 2015 Harvard Business Review reported that execution was the No. 1 challenge cited by global CEOs, topping innovation, geopolitical instability, and top-line growth.

Executing means getting things done, walking the talk and making things happen. It involves discipline and follow-up. Consider Benjamin Franklin's quote: "If you want something done, ask a busy person." We know who and what companies get things done.

According to Joe Clark, founder and CEO of Prana Business in Denver, Colorado, 90 per cent of U.S. companies that fail do so because they fail to execute. Clark created a diagnostic tool called Line-of-Sight for better strategy execution. Designed to give companies insights into how well employees are equipped to execute, it allows executives and their teams to make the necessary refinements for better execution.

We can have all the plans and good intentions in the world, but until we do something with it, it's irrelevant. Actions speak louder than words. I would estimate that at least 90 per cent of great strategic reports never get implemented. They just end up on the shelf gathering dust, or sitting on a server or in the cloud taking up space. The easy part is deciding what should be done. The difficult part is making the tough decisions and doing it. This involves:

+ Setting deadlines
+ Holding people accountable
+ Learning
+ Trying new things
+ Following up
+ Measuring

TRACKING AND MEASURING PERFORMANCE

Research shows that tracking your results and progress, and being accountable, doubles your results. Setting expectations by clearly articulating your goal is the first step in creating a culture of accountability.

As Paul Niven, author of Balanced Score Card Step-by-Step, says, "Three year total returns to shareholders are three times higher at companies where employees understand corporate objectives, and the ways in which their jobs contribute to achieving them."

A balanced score card includes four key parts:

1. Create concise statements about your goals, expectations and the desired outcomes. What does the company need to do well

---

to execute on its strategy? For example, one answer would be "To increase trust with customers in region ABC."

2. Measure it. How will we know we have done it? In other words, how will we know we have increased customer trust? In this example, one could measure it using the Client Trust Index™.

3. What target are we trying to achieve? Are we trying to achieve a Client Trust Index™ score of 80, 85, 95 or 100?

4. What strategic initiatives will we take to achieve our goal and desired outcome?

Strategy and a balanced score card are set at the highest levels of an organization. Objectives and key results come in at the execution level. Paul Niven is also the co-author of Objectives and Key Results (OKRs), which he wrote with Ben Lamorte. When I asked him about OKRs, he said, "90 per cent of the DNA of objectives and key results, and balanced score, overlap."

According to Niven, OKRs are best at the execution level throughout an organization. Execution takes place every day and you need to be agile. "Cadence is difference, you change OKRs every 90 days. OKRs are about asking, 'What do I need to do this quarter to optimize key results?' It stops there. Strategy and balanced score card is long term."

In Niven's experience, companies invest in OKRs because they want to more effectively execute strategy, and to do that they need to be more agile. Typically, companies adjust OKRs every quarter. Strategy is not adjusted on a regular basis, but typically once a year.

As we know, sharing the results and progress with employees and customers builds trust. And it goes without saying tracking and measuring performance must occur on a regular basis.

STRENGTHENING CUSTOMER TRUST FOR A DIGITAL MEDIA ICT SERVICES FIRM

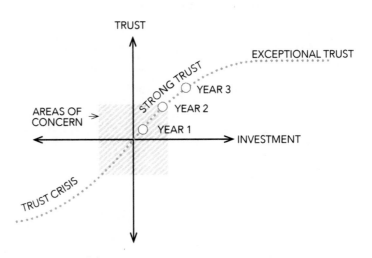

As has been stated, a large percentage of companies fail simply because they don't execute on their strategy. One hundred per cent of companies, regardless of industry or market, have a customer strategy whether they know it or not.

One of my clients, a Digital Media ICT services firm, who shall remain anonymous has been tracking their customer Trust Equity using the Client Trust Index™ for three years. They have been executing on their customer strategy, tracking and measuring their results.

Their customer strategy is built on customer value. They are delivering value, customer trust is increasing, the brand is flourishing and revenues have increased.

INNOVATION

Improving and innovating products and service offerings builds and protects trust. Keeping a product or a service offering up to date and free of defects, demonstrates that an organization is competent and committed. Every organization, regardless of industry, can demonstrate innovation.

Examples of innovation in business include:

- Providing menu choices that are gluten, dairy and/or nut free
- Displaying real time data and reports to customers
- Adding guest books and photo galleries to the obituary section of a funeral home website
- Installing Wi-Fi enabled cameras to construction job sites so customers can view the progress of their new building

CNN DELIVERS ON ITS PROMISE

CNN is an example of an organization that stays true to delivering on its promise of "getting the story right." The news organization is innovating by the use of drones in its coverage strategies.

As told to me by Greg Agvent, senior director of news at CNN, "We believe in compelling images that speak for themselves, high quality production value, unique story telling and powerful news. We use drones to provide another view of a story or a news event to our viewers and users. Drones are a very powerful tool. With our 35 years of ethical standards, we have strict standards and rules we adhere to. We spent 18 months developing our operations manual (on handling drones). We want to use our drones to cover the news, not to be the news."

ANTICIPATING, MEETING AND EXCEEDING EXPECTATIONS

Delivering on your promise is also about serving, anticipating, meeting and exceeding expectations. As Dennis Campbell, president and CEO of Ambassatours GrayLine says, "Only promise what you can deliver and honour your word."

What people want most from their boss, their supplier and their partner is similar to what children want from their parents, teachers, coaches and role models. They want care, appreciation and clear consistent expectations. Outlining and meeting expectations increases our confidence and trust in an organization. When it comes to articulating expectations there are three main components of expectations to address:

1. **Time:** How long will it take? Of my time, your time, and for the entire process? In other words, when will it be completed? Be specific. If it will take five days to complete, say five days.

2. **Investment:** How much will it cost? Or what are the fees? How many internal resources will it use to complete this? If there are no fees, say no fees. If there is a fee, make sure you let them know what it is. A sure way to lose trust is to send a bill that the customer is not expecting.

3. **Outcome:** What will the outcome be? What will we accomplish? What will the result be? What objective will be met? Be specific. For example, when an insurance transaction is complete, you will have a new account set up and you will have life insurance.

If one of these components is missing, the customer loses confidence. In addition, it goes without saying, we must do what we say we are going to do, what the customer expects and what we promise. Companies and organizations that do this are rated as reliable and trustworthy.

It is worth noting that 100 per cent of my research participants indicated reliability was the number one criterion in building trust.

*Does everyone in your organization
know the organization's key objectives,
the purpose and the promise?*

~

*Do they have the skills and capabilities
to deliver on their promises?*

Principle 8

Commit to the Long Term

Trust is assessed and reassessed continually over time through our experiences. Organizations and leaders must continually and deliberately work to create, earn and generate trust. Leaders will build trust, or alternatively tear it down, based on the cumulative actions they take, the words they speak and how they serve. A strong leader is committed and enthusiastic. This behaviour will rub off on colleagues, and customers and stakeholders will ultimately benefit.

> *"Enthusiasm is one of the most powerful engines of success. When you do a thing, do it with all your might. Put your whole soul into it. Stamp it with your own personality. Be active, be energetic, be enthusiastic and faithful, and you will accomplish your object. Nothing great was ever achieved without enthusiasm."*
>
> *– Ralph Waldo Emerson*

To be committed to the long-term means being enthusiastic and disciplined about creating a customer centred culture of trust, which includes:

+ Assessing and reassessing critical trust points
+ Training all employees on the importance of building trust
+ Ensuring the organization has appropriate values in place
+ Ensuring the organization has the appropriate policies and processes in place
+ Tracking and measuring performance
+ Sharing information, all types of information

♦   Providing training and orientation for new and existing employees so they
    understand the culture, vision, objectives and competencies of the organization

The better understanding an organization has of trust and the strength of the culture of trust, the more successful the organization will be at protecting and building
trust externally. If trust is deemed foundational and implicit, and the importance of
trust becomes top of mind, generating trust with external stakeholders will have a
higher degree of success.

As with all important activities, organizations must evaluate the results of their
trust building and protecting activities. Measuring how customers are reacting, on
a regular basis, exemplifies being committed to the long term.

EVERYONE IN THE ORGANIZATION NEEDS TO COMMIT

Two types of commitment are required to help make the choice to a long-term
relationship. The first is an executive's commitment to building a customer-focused trust culture. When this choice is made (and it is a choice), it must be
made at the senior executive level. At least one executive needs to be the champion or sponsor. The second part is a commitment from the employees, who make
it happen for customers every day.

At Kohltech Windows and Entrance Systems, the leader in commitment is
Kevin Pelley, the CEO and in many ways, the chief customer officer. Kohltech
is one of North America's leading window and door manufacturers. Window
specialty stores, contractors, installers and building suppliers across Canada and
the United States trust Kohltech. Everyone in the company is committed to their
customers and their industry, as well as continuous improvement, innovation and
product development. Not surprisingly, when the Client Trust Index™ was conducted, the company earned a high score.

Kohltech demonstrates its long-term commitment to customers in multiple ways, including hosting what they call "Kohltech University" several times a year. The company invites customers to corporate headquarters in Debert, Nova Scotia for two days. While there, customers receive training, tour the plant, meet the people who make it all happen, see the new products first hand and meet others in the industry. This type of service and commitment goes a long way with customers, especially in a world where many manufacturers are eliminating their travelling sales representatives and instead directing customers to a website for information.

Steven Bronken, vice president of sales and marketing at Safety Net Access, goes the extra mile to demonstrate that he is committed to his customers, suppliers and partners for the long term. Whether it is responsiveness in different time zones to deliver on a promise or learning to say thank you in his customer's native language.

COMMITMENT IN VARIOUS FORMS

There are many different types of commitment. Piotr Sztompka, a Polish sociologist and author of Trust: A Sociological Theory, outlined three types relating to trust: anticipatory, responsive and evocative. All types of commitment involve doing the right thing, depending on the situation you are in.

Anticipatory trust means an individual trusts and anticipates that another individual will do a good job. One person believes what another person does will be favourable to their interests, needs and expectations. This involves little commitment by both parties. This trust is often anticipated based on the individual's role. For example, we trust that a teacher will fulfill his role of teaching students, or a lawyer will do a good job of representing her clients. This type of commitment is aligned with Principle 7: Deliver on your Promise.

Responsive trust involves commitment of an expected response. This includes allowing someone to take care of something the trustor cares about. It implies obligation. Examples include trusting an office colleague to complete a project over a particular time, or trusting that an organization will publish its financial results on schedule. This type of commitment is aligned with the elements in Principle 4 Be Consistent: Predictable and Reliable.

In **evocative trust**, one person acts on the belief that another person will reciprocate their trust. The individual does what they say they are going to do in anticipation that the other person will as well. This type of commitment is aligned with the elements of Principle 7: Deliver On Your Promise. Actions match words. For example, if an individual says he will make a telephone call to introduce you to someone on his behalf, he fully intends to do so.

The above-mentioned types of commitments, or variations, are usually found within the phenomenon of trust. As mentioned, there are elements of commitment throughout many of the principles, most notably, principles Do the Right Thing, Act in the Customer's Best Interest, Deliver on Your Promise and Commit to the Long Term.

COMMITTING TO THE LONG TERM STARTS WITH BUILDING A CUSTOMER CENTRED TRUST CULTURE

In 2017, I contributed to a list of do and don'ts for a poster created by Trust Across America Alliance Members and other Top Thought Leaders in Trust. The title of the poster was Do and Don'ts To Foster Organizational Trust. Some of the dos below come from that poster. They are keys to building a culture of trust in your organization.

Do:

- Act from the belief that trust can be measured for its impact on business outcomes

- Lead by example

- Trust yourself first if you want people to trust you

- Share information about yourself. When you show vulnerability and reciprocity, you build connections and strengthen relationships of trust

- Make sure everyone in the organization is clear on the organization's purpose, vision and values

- Ensure all goals are mutually shared

- Get to know your colleagues and the people you lead, and treat everyone with the same degree of respect

- Praise frequently and show gratitude

- Include colleagues and stakeholders in the "how" and "why" of decision making

- Apologize when you do not meet your commitments

- Admit openly when you do not have the answer

- See your actions through other's eyes. Ask yourself, "Will I be perceived as promoting or eroding trust by this specific action?"

- Raise issues of trust, welcome constructive feedback from your colleagues, and encourage the same in return

- Keep team commitments even if you disagree

- Ask questions to develop mutual understanding and empathy

- Examine your organization's customer service policies to see if they build or erode trust

- Discuss the Eight Principles of Trust with colleagues

- Always ask: "How will this affect the customer?"

- Make customer concerns a priority

- Act in the best interests of your customers, employees, and stakeholders

- Remember that every employee makes an impact on a customer's decision to trust

- Remember that having a culture of trust inside your organization is your hidden asset

- Appreciate the level of trust customer's have in your organization to be the most important key performance indicator (KPI)

ORGANIZATIONAL POLICIES ENHANCE A CULTURE OF TRUST: EMPIRICAL STUDY OF TWO PROFESSIONAL SERVICES FIRMS

As we have noted, many scholars have written about trust and its benefits to organizational effectiveness. In the first study of its kind, scholars Frédérique Six and Arndt Sorge empirically investigated how organizations generate and enhance interpersonal trust by organizational policies. In their 2008 paper, Creating A High Trust Organization, they compared two Dutch professional services with different organizational policies. One firm has a deliberate policy of building interpersonal trust and the other does not.

The research is analyzed through the lens of relational signaling theory (RST). RST asserts that human behaviour is guided by the social rules within an organizational context. Several trust scholars argue that relational signals play a critical role in interpersonal trust building. The authors hypothesize that organizations can enhance interpersonal trust by focusing on relational signaling, instilling norms and reviewing their practices.

The authors used a qualitative, mixed method approach, which included in-depth interviews and quantitative methods, such as questionnaire surveys. Interviewees were asked about the culture of their organization and survey participants answered questions about actions on a five-point scale. The findings demonstrated that four organizational policies can be effective in generating interpersonal trust:

1. Creation of a culture that values relationships, such as care and concern for others
2. Facilitation of relational signaling among colleagues
3. Definitive training for new employees to understand the organization's values
4. Management and development of employee's professional competencies

The authors conclude that employees at firms with these policies were better able to create a trusting culture.

Committing to the long term requires passion, perseverance and a drive to improve. Angela Lee Duckworth, professor of Psychology at the University of Pennsylvania, calls this grit. In her book, Grit: The Power of Passion and Perseverance she shares her research about successful people. Her research reveals that the determining factor to success is the power of perseverance, hard work and a drive to improve. Being successful requires grit and commitment.

As Nike founder and CEO Phil Knight said in his autobiography, Shoe Dog, the best advice he ever gave himself was "just keep going. Don't stop. Don't even think about stopping until you get there..." He gave himself this advice in 1962. And in his autobiography 50 years later, he wrote, "Half a century later, I believe it's the best advice — maybe the only advice — any of us should ever give."

My advice to you is to never stop building trust with your customers, employees, colleagues and stakeholders. Never stop applying the Principles of Trust to your relationships.

Ten ways to demonstrate your commitment to the long term:

1. Show you appreciate customer and stakeholder relationships

2. Remember what is important to your customers, including the little things

3. Provide value and keep in touch after the sale is made or the project is finished

4. Be passionate about your customer's business

5. Train your employees to ensure customers receive the highest quality products and services

6. Seek feedback proactively

7. Be deliberate in how you communicate, behave and serve

8. Build a culture of trust within your organization every single day

9. Measure customer trust, and incorporate it as a key performance indicator (KPI)

10. Remember every customer wants what you promise to deliver

A clear sense of purpose
supported by a culture of trust
increases performance.

CASE STUDY

A Century of Trust
the Key to IBM's Success

IBM is often referred to as a company that "needs no introduction." Recently IBM was introduced as "the company that all technology companies want to grow up to be like." Something else we often hear: "no matter how complicated the project is, choose IBM, they can get it done and it will be done right."

IBM is one of the world's most trusted brands. We trust companies that are committed to the long term, companies that have a solid track record of success and companies we are familiar with. IBM's track record is 100 years long. Around the world the brand exudes professionalism, confidence, quality, excellence, innovation and commitment. IBM's commitment shows up in everything it does.

I recently sat down with one of IBM's Trust Leaders, Lisa Burke, Vice President GBS Global Delivery Excellence. I will never forget what Lisa said to me the first time we met: "I, along with many other executives at IBM are passionate about IBM, because IBM has the ability to change the world." She went on to say that, "Innovation is core to who we are. We are passionate about learning and innovation."

I also met John Wheeler, Vice President for security and also an IBM Trust Leader who is passionate about innovation. He shared with me that IBM invests $6.3 billion a year in research and development; has a 23-year track record of patent leadership; and

CASE STUDY

holds the largest patent portfolio of any company in the world. IBM walks the talk on innovation.

Commitment to Innovation

Lisa and I discussed IBM's acquisition of The Weather Company Product & Technology businesses. "It always starts with the customer," she said. "We want to help customers out-think, forecast and predict behaviors and trends through data and analytics. For example if we know there will be sun and fine weather on July 4 in the Midwest USA, we can let our retail customers know to move inventory and stock barbeque charcoal and outdoor items to that region of the country. When we listen by analytics we can improve the level of how we service our customers."

The company demonstrates its commitment to innovation in its support of the technology industry. In Atlanta, for example, IBM sponsors technology forums and contests. "We invest significant amounts across the world sponsoring innovation, we build out our ecosystems of suppliers and developers and we do a lot of work in our local communities to sponsor the innovators outside of IBM."

Regular Consistent Communication from the Leadership Team

Employees are in a strong position to create trust when they understand the company's vision, its' priorities and hold common values. I asked Lisa how a culture of innovation and learning is maintained in a firm with 380,000 employees and operations in 170-plus coun-

CASE STUDY

tries. How does the leadership team communicate priorities? Lisa told me about 'Think Academy' and how they communicate and involve employees in the strategy.

"One way is through 'Think Academy'," she said. "On a daily basis Think Academy sends us thought provoking information including news items, customer stories, links to videos, broadcasts from CEO Ginni Rometty. This enables continuous learning. We work at building learning into all of our customer solutions. It is also an effective vehicle to keep the fundamental messages in front of people."

As Lisa explained, many IBM employees are mobile, they don't go into an office, there are many different units so sometimes it is difficult to stay involved with their peers. "In Atlanta, we brought our Atlanta-based employees together through executive led 'what, why and how sessions.' We brought people together once a month over a few months to discuss strategy and what does that strategy mean to you in your particular role? We discussed and shared customer issues and experiences."

"We take our promises and commitment to our customers seriously, that is our number one tenet"

"Everything we do is centered around the customer." For example, "We focus on agile development and thinking and have agile champions across the company. How do you lower the center of gravity; push decision-making downward; increase speed and agility; simplify complicated things; make things easier for our employees and our customers; and empower employees?"

Employee trust increases when employees are empowered to make decisions to do the right thing for the customer.

CASE STUDY

Commitment to Excellence, Quality and Delivering on its Promise

Lisa's Global Business Services team focuses on supporting IBM teams worldwide in following best delivery practices. "We are committed to ensuring that the right technical expertise and leadership is involved to solve customer issues." They also work with IBM teams and customers around the world "to ensure that IBM is executing from a delivery perspective what it has promised to customers and to the IBM Corporation." Practically speaking, this may involve: deep program reviews and cadences with teams, applying new methodologies or processes, reviewing financial performance, advising teams on leadership and skills changes required, and meeting with customers.

Continuous Transformation, Commitment to Top Talent to Serve Customers

In the last 30 years IBM has gone through multiple transformations. As Ginni Rometty says: "When you stop transforming you will die." As Lisa said, "Technology is changing so rapidly, our customers are having to move at lightning speed. As our customers are shifting we are shifting." Much has been written about IBM's track record of successful transformations and its ability to help customers transform. In fact in June 2016 it was named one of the world's Top 4 in the list of 100 influential brands in digital transformation by Onalytica.

Part of IBM's transformation is hiring new skills and new people to spur on continual innovation. In 2015 IBM hired tens

CASE STUDY

of thousands of new employees, which included people from 14 acquisitions. Part of IBM's brand is to hire top talent and to invest in people. In some IBM divisions, for example, new employees go through a two-year orientation and training program.

After 28 years at IBM in various roles, Lisa has a lot of stories, lessons and advice to share. She has lived and worked with IBM in Asia and in North America and has been involved in customer projects all over the world. I asked her to tell me about something that makes her proud of her company.

"When you look at some of the things we do in partnership with our customers, it is hard not to get emotional about the impact of our business at times. To think about what we have done in health care, through our Watson business, as an example, is amazing. Part of what I love about IBM is that we have impacted people's lives, through changing the way they live. Another example, we have sent teams to Africa to support the development of an effective water treatment system, as an investment in the community, and as an investment in the teams that we send, again changing people's lives. IBMers have pride in what we do. Yes, it is about returning a profit to our shareholders but there is so much more to IBM quite frankly."

IBM's vision and its culture of innovation, growth and commitment are at the core of its trust brand. It is people and leaders like Lisa Burke that make IBM one of the world's most trusted brands.

CASE STUDY

Highlights from this case study

- Innovation demonstrates commitment to the long term
- "Everything we do is centered around the customer."
- Process and controls to ensure the focus on delivering quality and excellence
- Walk the talk, if you focused on innovation, invest in it
- Empower regions and people to better serve the customer
- Commitment to hiring top talent demonstrates commitment to long term
- Investment in learning and development of employees
- Demonstrate value of innovation through supporting technology and innovation outside of the company
- Frequent communication of company vision and goals from the Leadership team to employees, regardless of the size of the company

6

Protecting Your
Trust Equity

The Eight Principles of Building, Strengthening and Protecting Trust are not a set of rigid rules. The trust model and the Eight Principles are intended to be used as a framework to enhance relationships with customers, suppliers, employees and stakeholders.

Applying the principles of trust every day creates trusting relationships and moments of trust. Building and strengthening trust takes time. It is the culmination of multiple experiences and events with a company, its employees, its customers and stakeholders. It is about one person, one department, one division, one region, one country at a time.

These principles are interconnected. Applying them consistently creates a culture that inspires trust. This creates momentum.

Empirical testing of my model demonstrates that when organizations apply the Eight Principles their Client Trust Index™ score improves. You reap the rewards when customer trust becomes a key performance metric and applying the Eight Principles becomes part of how you practice business.

It is an incremental process. Resolve each day to put it into practice. As the saying goes, practice makes perfect. As author Malcolm Gladwell asserted in his book

Outliers, ten thousand hours is the magic number of greatness. I would recommend you consider acknowledging or taking note of how you applied the principles to build, strengthen or protect trust at the end of each day.

THE SIGNIFICANCE OF TIME - HOW TIME CAN IMPACT TRUST

When we conduct the Client Trust Index™ we often add a qualifying question to determine how long the customer has been in a relationship with the organization. We compare the Client Trust Index™ scores by length of the relationship. A clear pattern is discernible in this, regardless of industry, type of business or size of sample.

We noticed it first when we were working with an ICT services company that has been in business for about 16 years. Results showed that overall, customers who had a relationship with the company for less than three years had a stronger Client Trust Index™ score than any other segment. There was a distinct dip in the trust equity with customers in relationships from three to 10 years and then a rise in the score when the relationship had been in place for 10 or more years.

Client Trust Index™ by Length of Relationship

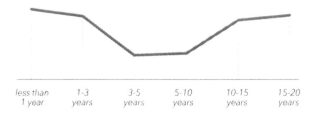

| less than 1 year | 1-3 years | 3-5 years | 5-10 years | 10-15 years | 15-20 years |

We have since seen the same pattern again and again: with various types and sizes of companies, from manufacturing and hospitality companies, to professional services and software development firms. Academics have been researching and writing about the lifecycle of the customer relationship for years. Many refer to the early stages of the relationship as the honeymoon phase.

Let's try to understand this better by looking at the phenomenon from the customer's point of view.

The customer's trust in the company is high when buying a product or service, or starting work on a project. They have completed due diligence and most likely feel good about the decision.

The company is likely paying a lot of attention to the new customer, investing a lot of time and effort and both sides are getting to know each other. Trust is building. They are following up on initial shipments, installs, reports or projects and there is a lot of interaction. Many companies ask for feedback after the initial sale. It's usually positive for both sides in the initial stages. Some companies have established well-documented processes to welcome and integrate new customers. Some of my clients refer to this as 'onboarding stage' while others refer to it as the 'orientation stage'.

Following this honeymoon period, everyone (customers and company employees) starts to get comfortable with each other. To use the marriage metaphor, "the honeymoon is over," although everything might be just fine. Most of us know what this means. In a marriage or a personal relationship, we might become a bit less conscientious, thoughtful, attuned to the other person's needs, or as compassionate as we were in the beginning. Maybe we forget to put our lipstick on, fail to bring flowers home or pick up our socks from the middle of the bedroom floor.

Similar things happen with customer relationships. In companies, it is often referred to as maintenance, ongoing support or annual transaction mode. Companies stop paying attention to the customer. Sometimes they are taken for granted. We have to watch for this because we have to continue earning customer trust.

It's also about protecting the trust you have built. Every once in a while, we need to bring the flowers home or the chocolates or have the date nights, even if there is no reason other than to let the person know they are appreciated. Trust builds based on the cumulative experiences. Trust is also protected based on cumulative experiences.

Time allows customers to get to know a company, to experience it in multiple situations, positive and negative, good times and bad, carefree and stressful. My research indicates that in very long relationships of 20 years or more, trust can be at its greatest. Here is an example from my consulting practice:

Client Trust Index™ by Length of Relationship

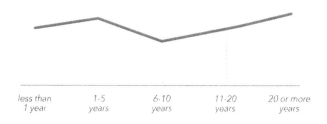

| less than 1 year | 1-5 years | 6-10 years | 11-20 years | 20 or more years |

The Client Trust Index™ score improves with length of time. Why? Do customers feel nostalgic? Or is it like the old saying, old friends are the best friends? Or could it be that we forget all the difficult stressful times, the mistakes and the problems and are grateful that the relationship has endured 20 years? Perhaps the status quo is simply more comfortable than change, or that people want to continue doing business with friends. Many of us do business with neighbours, university or childhood friends. Every case is different. It might be that the relationships last just because everyone knows everyone else so well and they feel connected.

Sometimes shortcomings can be overlooked or put in perspective because of the trust equity that has been built.

+ Time adds stability to the relationship
+ Time engenders familiarity
+ Time enables investments to appreciate
+ Time increases the trust equity you have with the customer

> The challenge is for organizations to protect and maintain the trust equity they have with customers. As we've noticed, there is often a dip in the Client Trust Index™ score during the fifth to tenth years of a business relationship. But organizations have a significant corporate advantage when they protect and strengthen trust.

WHO IS RESPONSIBLE FOR PROTECTING AND MAINTAINING TRUST WITH CUSTOMERS?

The simple answer is everyone. Yes, everyone in the organization is responsible for building, protecting and strengthening trust with customers. When we peel the onion on responsibility, we find that the responsibility is actually dichotomous. It is the senior leadership and the front line employees who interact with customers and the people outside the organization. The focus on the importance of trust with customers, suppliers and stakeholders is the responsibility of the senior executive team; however, the actual day to day execution of it and how trust is actually built comes down to the front line people who are having the interactions and experiences with the customers every day.

The customer's trust in the organization is made up of the sum of the experiences they have with everyone in the company.

CUSTOMER TOUCH POINTS

Customer touch points range right across the business relationship. It could be seeing the CEO on TV, hearing a VP speak at an event, a visit by a technician to your home or office, visiting a retail store or a website, interacting with a call centre or online through social media, to the user interface on your customer portal, or the way the bill or invoice looks.

Heather Tulk, a former senior vice president of Bell Canada, and former Chief Customer Officer for MTS Allstream, says "Whether you are the CEO, the installer who pulls wire in a home to bring you broadband, the customer service representative on the other end of the telephone, the sales clerk at The Source, a sales clerk at a Bell kiosk in a shopping mall, the manager of the largest fleet of vehicles in Canada or a truck driver or receptionist, everyone affects trust." As Heather says, "The biggest way we can improve trust with our customers is to consistently improve our customer experience."

The experiences we have with front line staff have a significant impact on the organization's trust equity. Pierre Cléroux, vice president of research and chief economist of Business Development Bank of Canada says, "The bank's account managers are critical to building and preserving client trust." Susan Helstab, formerly of Four Seasons Hotels and Resorts says, "All guest-facing employees are key to earning the customers trust." Dennis Campbell, CEO of Ambassatours GrayLine offers a similar comment: "The bus drivers, in many cases, are the face of the company." Scott McCain, former COO of Maple Leaf Foods and director of McCain Foods says, "The marketing team on the sell side and buying on the purchasing side is responsible for creating trust with external publics."

As one of my clients, a managing partner in a successful accounting firm says, "From the managing partners to the junior accountants to the preparers, we are all focused on the customer and we are all responsible for delivering a high quality product and service to our customers." Another client of mine says, "it's about the IT support, the sales engineers, the project managers and then the account managers."

In every industry, and at every company, the front line staff or customer facing staff is critical to protecting trust with customers.

Practical Ways to Apply the Eight Principles
of Building, Strengthening and Protecting Trust

Principle 1

Listen carefully with empathy and compassion,
question and involve your customers in dialogue

- Remember customers are people, and every customer has their own issues. Be compassionate. Ask yourself, "How can I truly help them?" Conduct a "learn about the customer" event in your company to increase empathy
- Share customer stories inside your organization to build understanding
- Introduce the customer or customer organization to staff members so they can understand customer's priorities, situation and purpose. For example, if you are an engineering firm, explain the customer situation to colleagues working on the file
- Place the customer's name on the product you are making so everyone in the company knows which customer the product is being made for. For example, manufacturers can add a note or a label to a product as it goes through the production process that outlines the customer's name, situation, issues, and how and where it will be used
- Spend time understanding what your customer's business objectives are
- Offer information about yourself to share and demonstrate similarities, and build the connection with customers
- Use the word "we" more, and the word "I" less
- Ask three additional questions at the end of the purchase decision conversation
- Ask for specifics
- Ask "Why?"
- Ask "Is there anything else we need to know about your needs or issues?"

- Seek first to understand, then to be understood
- Ask questions to understand what it is like to be in your customer's situation. Mutual understanding and empathy strengthen relationships of trust
- Turn your phone off when you are talking to someone; show them that you are listening to them. Glancing at the phone says to the other person, "She is thinking about something else and isn't interested in this any more"
- Engage customers in conversation, preferably face-to-face. Close alternatives, however not as affective, include videoconference. Zoom is my favourite video and web conferencing service. Telephone is the next best thing followed by social media, email and letters. Handwritten letters are personal and more effective than email and social media. They communicate thoughtfulness.
- Hold town hall meetings to solicit feedback and discuss issues
- Conduct focus groups
- Monitor social media
- Survey customers
- Follow customer news
- Participate in online discussions
- Involve customers in social media; encourage them to post feedback about their experiences with you, your employees and your products
- Hold briefing meetings
- Understand what your customer's particular sensitivities are. For example, are they most concerned about deadlines, price, quality, changes in plans, disruptions, safety, security breaches, public opinion, labour, employee relations or the relationships they have with their customers?
- Demonstrate patience

Two organizations that do this exceptionally well and how they do it:

1. **The Canadian Medical Association** (CMA) is an example of an organization that successfully listened to its customers, in this case members were the customers. The CMA represents more than 85,000 physicians and is considered the voice of Canadian doctors. To speak with a unified voice, however, requires expert listening skills — skills the association is always working to sharpen. According to John Feeley, vice-president of member relevance, "We continually strive to find ways to listen and engage with the members we represent."

The CMA deals with a lot of difficult and controversial issues, such as medical assistance in dying, so it needs good engagement skills. Over a four-year period from 2012 to 2016, the CMA employed several channels and tools to consult with its members and ensure it was accurately representing their best interests.

These channels and tools included:
- Face-to-face member town hall meetings
- Several member surveys
- Opportunities for online engagement, including a discussion forum
- Direct email communications

By June 2016, federal legislation on medical assistance in dying was passed which closely followed the recommendations that the CMA developed in consultation with its membership. But the work didn't end there. The CMA committed to continued study of the new legislation and its impact on physicians and their patients.

To prepare physicians to respond to the end-of-life care wishes of their patients, the CMA developed two educational programs on end-of-life care and medical assistance in dying: a foundational online course, free of charge for members, and a more in-depth face-to-face program for physicians who might wish to provide this service. The CMA is committed to providing ongoing support to its members now that medical assistance in dying is part of medical practice in Canada.

2. BMW involves customers in driving events and encourages customers to post pictures of themselves online with their cars.

Principle 2

Communicate using clear, concrete and conversational language

---

- Remember, simplicity builds trust
- Communicate conversationally
- Use examples to make your point
- Strive to tighten the language you are using
- Introduce visuals, metaphors and deeper explanations
- Increase the frequency of your communication
- Clearly articulate your strategy, vision, goals and interests
- Avoid acronyms and industry jargon
- Offer context and explanation. Answer the "Why?"
- Be specific. Avoid vague statements
- Identify the customers' most frequently asked questions and communicate them to the employees, document them and share them with customers
- Identify what issues customers are most concerned about
- Break your plan into phases, and introduce milestones
- Pay attention to your own body language. Are the messages you are sending the ones you want your customers to receive? For example, watch for signals that communicate impatience and lack of empathy, such as looking at a watch, phone or device, shaking your head while listening, responding to the customer with dismissive comments like "Right" or "Sure," or asking how much time will this take
- Avoid abbreviated names for your company and its products

- Remember that visual learners constitute 55 per cent of the population, 30 per cent are kinesthetic and 15 per cent are auditory learners
- Be aware that sports analogies only work in cultures where the sport is played, and with people who know and understand the sport
- Be aware there are different social styles
- Put down your pen when you're talking to a customer or close your laptop or tablet, unless you are using it to take notes
- Test your messages with someone who knows nothing about your company

Two companies that do this exceptionally well and how they do it

1. Google. They "simplify search" for users. It is so simple and clear it has become a verb. My 79-year-old father is continually telling me to "Just Google it." As he said, "I never read any instructions on how to use Google and I went on it and it works. You just have to use it once and you know it is as simple as they say it is."

2. Wal-mart. They have clear concise messages. They promise "everyday low prices" and "the best value for the money." Their behaviour "walks the talk."

Principle 3

Be Honest and Transparent

- Evaluate your company information for accuracy, vagueness and clarity
- Do not exaggerate your qualifications, the benefits of your product or services and the length of time required to provide them
- Check facts and timelines. Are they accurate? Do they set realistic expectations?
- Declare any perceived and real conflicts of interest
- Do not deliberately omit relevant information
- Respect confidences and confidentially agreements
- Inform customers of personnel or process changes that might affect them
- If another company would do a better job than you, tell the customer that
- Share information about yourself. When you show vulnerability and reciprocity, it strengthens trust
- Share important truths even if they are unpleasant
- Disclose information that may affect the project or your business relationship
- Disclose the challenges of your industry and of your company
- Share timelines
- Point out potential negative consequences, for example, say, "This might cost more" or "We might face delays"
- Identify uncomfortable questions and prepare responses
- Anticipate that your customer might ask, "Is there anything else I should know that you haven't told me?" or "Is there any reason why we should not choose your company?" or "If you were me, what would you do?" or "What would you recommend your mother or child to do?"

Two companies that do this really well and how they do it:

1. The Economist Magazine. The New York Times describes it as the most trusted new magazine in the English-speaking world. The Economist publishes its mistakes, specifically if what they published was factually wrong.

2. CSX Corporation is one of North America's leading transportation suppliers. The company provides rail-based transportation services. In 2017, it was recognized as having high integrity the most trusted publically traded companies in the U.S. by Trust Across America. The company strives to communicate with clear concrete language that is understandable and conversational.

They have created a "Railroad dictionary." This is a simple and effective method of making it easy to understand their industry. The tool also demonstrates its commitment to transparency, and acting in the public's best interests by making the information accessible.

Principle 4

Be Consistent, Predictable and Reliable

+ Evaluate the consistency of the customer interactions with customers
+ Strive to set and meet schedules, agenda and timelines
+ Review company policies and procedures. Are they consistent with values of the company?
+ Do follow up. Consistent follow-up communicates that you care and are organized. It reinforces a commitment to the relationship
+ Do not surprise your customers and colleagues. Predictability strengthens trust
+ Identify, acknowledge and continue rituals and traditions that are important to employees and customers
+ Organize your calendar and activities
+ Know about dates that are significant to your customer
+ Identify your customer's critical trust risk points, and plot them out
+ Attend customer meetings and presentations when appropriate
+ Audit the company's online brand

Two companies that do this well and how they do it:

1. Tim Hortons: The quality and price of a large coffee is the same across the entire country. They have consistent products, people, prices and locations. The donuts and the bagels taste the same in Vancouver, Montreal, Minneapolis or New York.

2. Coca-Cola Company: Invented by Dr. John S. Pemberton in 1886, the company protects the 'formula' for Coca-Cola fiercely. The taste, the feeling, the fizz and packaging is consistent wherever you buy a bottle or a can of Coke around the world. There are no surprises.

Principle 5

Act in the Best Interests of Your Customers, Stakeholders and the Public

- Make customer concerns your top priority
- Work within your customer's timeline
- Spend more time thinking about how a decision or policy will affect customers and stakeholders
- Find out what is the most important issue to your customer, such as deadlines, cost, follow ups, keeping appointments and being on time
- Determine the best way to communicate with your customer, by phone, text, email, Zoom, Snapchat, snail mail, Facetime, Facebook or face-to-face visits
- Offer customers advice that gets them the best value for their money, even if it means they may not use your product or service
- Respond to a customer promptly. Return phone calls, even if you are busy. Do it before you leave your office or finish for the day
- Continually think about issues from the customer's point of view
- Determine if there are other companies or professionals to whom you should or could introduce customers
- Educate customers about all of your products, services, policies, procedures, and your organization
- Publish recall notices
- Have a conflict of interest policy. Communicate and enforce it with employees
- Provide advice even when you are not compensated for it, and even if it might not directly be of financial benefit to you

- Introduce your customers to other solutions and options
- Involve customers in product and service development
- Align employee performance and incentives with customer satisfaction, commitment and customer trust in the company
- Recall or stop making products as soon as you realize there is an issue
- Take pictures of your customers and post them in your office to remind staff who their decisions will have an impact on
- Add customer stories to meeting agendas
- Research your customer's industry to provide the best advice
- Strive to deliver the highest quality, even if it costs you more
- Strive to empower employees to act in the customer's best interest
- Use your product or service as a customer would

Two companies that do this well and how they do it:

1. The retail clothing company Lululemon Athletica advises customers how to wash the product and to thoroughly check the item before buying it. Lululemon openly shares its values and the company's purpose and materials. It also promises alterations within 24 hours, or eight days if you do not live in the city. They will alter the clothing article purchased on the same day so that you can take it with you.

2. Orange Lake Resorts allows guests to sign out games and balls, and allows guests to bring snacks to the poolside at its resorts, even though it sells drinks and food at its pools. Its founder, Kemmons Wilson, also the founder of the Holiday Inn chain, wanted to offer great family resorts. The organization has stayed true to its values.

Principle 6

Do the Right Thing.
If you Make a Mistake, Fix it

- Document and discuss critical trust risk points with those affected on a regular basis
- Share your values, code of conduct and ethical standards
- Document and discuss examples of doing the right thing with employees
- Choose to engage in a fair process
- Fix mistakes in a way that you would be proud of
- Document and enforce a conflict of interest policy
- Create a process to resolve conflicts of interests internally
- Have a documented crisis communication plan
- Take actions that demonstrate your concern for customers
- Do not ignore customers, employees or stakeholder issues
- Do keep commitments
- If the project scope, price or personnel on the project changes, let the customer know

Two companies that do this really well and how they do it:

1. Nike was criticized for factory conditions in the early 2000s and made significant improvements. When Nike co-founder Phil Knight learned of it, he said, "We told ourselves we must do better." In shoe factories, the rubber room used to be one of the worst areas, environmentally.

Nike invented a water-based bonding agent to eliminate 97 per cent of carcinogens in the air. Then Nike gave the invention to all companies and factories in the shoe industry, even to their competitors. According to Knight, as stated in Shoe Dog, "Nearly all of them now use it. Today, the factories that make our products are among the best in the world. An official at the United Nations recently said so." Nike is now the gold standard by which we measure apparel factories. I would argue that their actions spoke louder than their words. It is also an example of how Nike demonstrates that it lives by its slogan, "Just do it."

2. Starbucks is committed to continuous improvement and it takes the time to understand customer feedback. In 2008, declining results showed that customers were not happy. Starbucks chairman and CEO, Howard Schultz, shut down 7,100 U.S. locations to conduct training, and 135,000 employees were trained to prepare drinks properly — the art of espresso.

"We are passionate about our coffee. And we will revisit our standards of quality that are the foundation for the trust that our customers have in our coffee and in all of us," Schultz wrote in a memo titled "Howard Schultz Transformation Agenda Communication #8."

Principle 7

Deliver on Your Promise

- Do give dates you can commit to, reconfirm
- Increase the focus on professional development and training for employees so they have the capabilities to deliver on the organization's promise
- Under-promise and over-deliver, not the other way around
- Share the company vision and its purpose with employees
- Follow up with customers on a regular basis
- Do not offer commitments that you cannot honour
- Schedule time to do what you say you are going to do
- Create check lists; spend time organizing your year, month, quarter, week, day and so on
- Hold colleagues and customers accountable
- Discuss key performance indicators in your company meetings
- Instill key performance indicators and/or objectives and key results discipline in your organization
- Discuss the company story and history with employees
- Have the sales reps do a presentation about a customer at every sales meeting
- Schedule follow-ups with customers after project is finished
- Publish and follow rules to keep your customer's information secure
- Hire and develop the right talent and skill sets
- Share industry news with employees and customers
- Invest in innovation
- Evaluate your company and its products and services from the customer's point

of view

- Follow up on customer requests and customer feedback
- Share the rewards with employees and customers
- Keep up to date with industry knowledge
- Strive to consistently learn and improve
- Consider employing a fact checker, or quality control person on staff
- Consider hiring an ombudsman on staff

Two companies that do this well and how they do it:

1. Ikea is a home furnishing retailer who promises to offer a wide range of products of "good design and function at prices so low, the majority of people can afford them." The company's 400 stores span 50 countries. Whenever the company is mentioned, I hear, "the product is good, and it is low cost." This is what the company has been promising since 1943.

2. Irving Oil's gas stations, restaurants and truck stops deliver on the promise of clean washrooms. They post a sign stating they promise clean bathrooms and a sheet on the back of the bathroom door that promises: "We check every 30 minutes." There is a list of items and space for an employee signature and time for each item. The time and signature are marked, so customers know it has been done. The sign says, "This is important to us. If you have an issue, please come see us."

Principle 8

Commit to the Long Term

- Regularly thank your customers for their business, loyalty and referrals
- Ask your customer, how can we be more helpful?
- Actively seek feedback on customer experiences
- Demonstrate your organization's passion for continuous improvement.
- Support the initiatives, projects and causes that are important to your customers, employees and communities
- Be a good corporate and community citizen
- Share information that could provide value, i.e. "In case you missed this..."
- Provide timely follow up for feedback on customer experience
- Broaden your perspectives; learn about your customers, and others in your industry
- Understand that trust takes time. For some customers, it takes years to develop
- Ask the following questions at your next team or department meeting: How can we improve our service? What do we do that frustrates the customer? Are we accessible?
- Ask you customers for feedback and if you receive some, use it to improve
- Make customer trust a key performance indicator (KPI)
- Initiate a policy for new customers; check in with them a week after your transaction and then in a month, send them a thank you for their business. Check in with them regularly. One of my customers asked me, how do you know how often? Every business is different. I would recommend checking in at least twice a year, no matter what business you are in.

+ Incorporate a discussion of trust into your meeting agenda
+ Send thank you notes to customers
+ Create objectives and key results that allow for steady progress
+ Identify customer touch points, and ask how they can be improved
+ Include the topic of customer touch points on the agenda of your next meeting
+ Ask customers for new product ideas

Two companies that do this well and how they do it:

1. Disney promises a magical experience. Across all of its parks, hotels, movies merchandise, cruises and resorts, they provide a "guest-focused" experience. The company is continuously innovating and improving the experiences and products they offer.

2. McDonald's: When you go to the history section on McDonald's website, it says: "Since 1955, we've proudly served the world some of its favourite food. It's been an exciting journey, and we're just getting started." This tells us they are in it for the long term.

McDonald's restaurants has demonstrated its commitment to the long term through its passion for continuous improvement, consistency, community involvement and innovation. It regularly updates its menus and restaurant spaces. McDonald's looks at its offerings from the customer's point of view and innovates to improve the customer service and overall experience.

In 2017, for example, McDonald's Canada has had three announcements that showcase its commitment to its customers and communities: in May it announced the celebration of McHappy Day, whereby $1 from sales of specific items across Canada support Ronald McDonald House; on July 4 it announced partnering with UberEATS to launch McDelivery service in three Canadian provinces and 187 restaurants; and at the end of July it announced the creation of a "McDonald's

Boombox." A McDonald's Boombox is made out of recyclable cardboard drink trays and was designed for customers to use as speakers for their smart phones and devices. They were made available for one day only for an event in Toronto.

In addition to its commitment to the long term, the company's focus on consistency, predictability and reliability makes McDonald's one of the world's most trusted brands. They have consistent products, people, processes, prices and locations. McDonald's French fries taste the same in Seattle, Montreal, London and Bejing.

7

Building Trust in the Online Minefield

There is nothing better than face-to-face interaction. Face to face is the most effective way to build trust. However, we can become more familiar with companies and get to know them better through their online presence. Many of us do our research online before we meet someone face to face. It is a critical customer touch point that every business should pay attention to. Your online presence, or lack of it, makes a statement.

Just as the introduction of the road changed our manner of transportation, trade and communication, social media has changed the way millions of people communicate, build relationships and access information.

Mark Zuckerberg, founder and chief executive officer of Facebook, stated in the letter to shareholders in the Facebook initial public offering in 2012, "Facebook has changed our relations to one another and to ourselves."

This is the new reality. Canadian communications scholar Marshall McLuhan became a global public figure more than a half a century ago by his assertion that "the medium is the message" that the medium itself is part of what we are trying to say. McLuhan teaches us that we can't escape the effects of a dominant medium of communication. The ubiquitous and participatory nature of social media has resulted in a sea change for companies and the relationships they have with customers and stakeholders.

An organization's online presence is a critical customer touch point that every organization, no matter the market, should nurture. Online presence, or a lack of it, demonstrates how a business communicates, behaves and serves customers. Your brand's digital footprint can create and maintain trust in your organization's reputation, or destroy it in the time it takes to play a video.

According to the 2014 and 2015 Edelman Trust Barometers:

- 65 per cent of Internet users view online searches as the most trusted source of information about companies
- 48 per cent share positive opinions online when they trust a company
- 37 per cent share negative opinions online when they do not trust

Access is one of the most significant changes brought about by the online business world. Traditional gatekeepers no longer exist. When an organization's news breaks, the public reports on it immediately and the reaction is instantaneous. In many cases, citizen journalists and social media influencers publish information faster than traditional media journalists, partly because conventional media tends to check information before it's published. But social media platforms can report on a story within seconds.

Everything you say, write or do online can instantly be made public. And as we know, everything on the Internet is a permanent, retrievable record. This gives us access to information, the organization and the employees that create a sense of familiarity. And familiarity can build trust. Yet feedback is close to instant and third party views of your company or product can strengthen or detract from a trusting relationship.

According to the 2015 Edelman Trust Barometer, 31 per cent of people trust sources they learn about from friends and academics more than they trust the company. The expectation is that organizations will respond immediately. How the company responds and when it responds affects its Client Trust Index™ score.

Social media has brought transparency to the forefront and ultimately highlighted the importance of trust. People are increasingly skeptical and more demanding; they expect truthful, timely and ethical communication and they trust organizations less. People demand transparency and accountability and are increasingly active online. We now live in a world where brands, large and small, can be attacked with a few strokes of the keyboard.

Communication scholars Linjuan Rita Men and Wan-Hsiu Sunny Tsai, both of the University of Miami, reported that there are three essential strategies for relationship cultivation on the Internet. They identified the strategies as: disclosure or openness, information dissemination and interactivity, and involvement. All three play active roles in maintaining and cultivating relationships. The conversational nature of social media allows for relationship cultivation. All types of organizations can communicate and build relationships with stakeholders using social media, whether they are large publicly traded multinational organizations, government departments, small businesses, or not-for-profit organizations. The Internet is a great equalizer in terms of relationship building.

Social media brings organizations more to the individual level. People interact with people rather than with organizations. Social media brings multiple faces to an organization. Before the advent of social media, people often associated the president, spokesperson or a few key employees with public or external roles with the organization. This is no longer the case. Social media allows an organization to have multiple connections to stakeholders. Each connection can play a role in building important relationships with stakeholders.

Consider these facts about credible company spokespersons (Edelman Trust Barometer, 2015):

- 70 per cent state the most credible spokesperson is an academic or industry expert, closely followed by a technical expert in the company (67 per cent)
- 63 per cent say they trust a person like themselves
- 47 per cent say the CEO is the least credible spokesperson

The survey also asked about spokespeople for specific types of information.

- Academics (37 per cent) were the most credible in relaying information about products, while media spokespeople are the least trusted at 13 per cent
- Employees rank as the No. 1 credible source for information about the engagement level of employees within the organization (47 per cent), and the organization's integrity (34 per cent)
- Employees and academics are tied at 31 per cent as the most trusted source for information about the company's operations
- Consumer activists (34 per cent) and academics (34 per cent) are the most credible spokespeople for a company when discussing the organization's purpose

People trust independent sources. They trust sources that are objective and do not have a vested interest in communicating anything but the facts. We believe people who are knowledgeable, well-informed and who act in the public's best interests, not just their own.

If your company employs academics, industry experts, scientists and technical experts that are recognized as thought leaders, they should be the primary spokespeople and content providers. This is especially true when discussing products and services. They are key to building trust with customers and external stakeholders. However, they must be well informed and empowered to communicate on the company's behalf. Are you leveraging their involvement in customer communications and stakeholder relations? Everyone in the company should be well informed because everyone has a part to play in building customer trust.

For organizations without academics or industry experts on staff, the endorsement of an outside academic or industry expert will build credibility for your organization. According to the Edelman 2015 Trust Barometer, content provided by friends and family is most trusted at 72 per cent, while content provided by company employees is trusted by 52 per cent.

What does this mean? It means people rarely believe advertising or company messages. We believe what our credible sources tell us. Essentially, customers, suppliers and employees are the company's most effective sales and spokespeople.

CODE OF CONDUCT ONLINE TO BUILD TRUST - DAVID ALSTON, TRUST LEADER

According to David Alston, a technology entrepreneur from Saint John, New Brunswick, "there is a certain code of conduct online to build trust."

David is the chief innovation officer for the data analytics company Introhive, advisor to multiple start-ups and a leader in building trust online. In 2014, Forbes named David one of 50 Influential chief marketing officers on social media and Social Media Magazine has consistently named him as a Top CMO on Twitter.

According to David, "You need to be real friends, meaning you need to be sincere and authentic. All standalone marketing is intention based. When you screw up, no one comes to your rescue. When people get to know people it represents their brand well. We [at Introhive, Radian 6 and Salesforce] spent a lot of time making deposits, sharing, thanking, making connections."

For David, building relationships comes down to investing deposits in "an emotional bank account." He shared a story about his early days at Radian 6, which is now part of Salesforce. They learned that a competitor was going to launch a product the same day Radian 6 was launching new features. "We wanted to make sure our news and our new features didn't get lost. So we wrote a song about the new feature and the community rewarded us. We posted the song and me singing the song on YouTube. It was a stretch for us and for me. It was a way of us reaching out to the online community for support. They came through; we had about 1,000 views, which was a lot. Our new features didn't get lost."

Building online trust includes making deposits. This includes taking the time to share information with people with similar interests and investing in relationships with them. Investing in relationships takes time, and as we know, investing in new relationships takes even more time.

One way to make a deposit is content marketing, which is important in building trust. "Giving away information helps create and build relationships. Community engagement is all about being a good neighbour, saying nice things, thanking your customers and people in your community," said David. "Trust is critical to start-ups."

Like the offline world, trust is built online through multiple interactions, sources and touch points, including websites, photos, images, case studies and third-party endorsements. Being part of the online community and being associated with other trustworthy people and organizations is important, as are online groups, comments, posts and articles.

Social media can be used as a powerful engine to achieve organizational goals, have a customer-focused culture online and apply the Eight Principles of building trust.

ADVICE FROM GREG AGVENT, TRUST LEADER, CNN

Greg Agvent, Senior News Director of CNN, says the way for brands to get on the most trusted list is simple: be honest in every area of your business. "Our product is consumed and we have constant feedback: ratings on TV, and online we have comments and discussion," says Greg. "We also have what we call 'war rooms', where we measure user and viewer feedback in real time. I would advise companies to engage with their consumers in the media in which they are using, most likely social media, in an open and honest way. I would also suggest you monitor and measure your reputation proactively."

Then I asked him, "How do you protect the trust you have with your viewers and users on digital platforms?" Greg told me "We build on our experiences. We are human, we have made mistakes, and we learn from them and fix them quickly. We have an ombudsman, an extremely engaged and active legal component to our business; we have fact checkers ... several layers of fact checkers. To us, we would rather 'have it right than first.' In the news business most want it first. We don't rush, it is more important to us to have it right. We have to have two sources and everything is approved at a senior level. If it is not an accepted news source we do not go forward. We vet constantly."

CNN is an example of a Trust Leader that applies the Principles of Trust to how it serves communicates and how it behaves. The consumer centred trust culture is woven into the fabric of how CNN operates.

Eight Steps to Build Trust Online

1. Be clear about your objectives. What are you trying to achieve? For example, an objective may be to share product updates; gather customer requirements; provide information about a topic that stakeholders are interested in; initiate or participate in discussions in order to communicate your company's opinion or experience on an issue. Create an online strategy that will achieve your organization's objectives.

2. Understand the stakeholders, their issues and where they are online. The more you know about your stakeholders, the more targeted and effective your online presence will be. What platforms are your customers using now? What is the best way to communicate your message? Is it video, podcast, pictures, diagrams or texts? A key part of your social technology selection is user experience, ease of use and customer experience.

3. Create clear key messages. Simplicity and clarity inspire trust. Make the content user-friendly. Follow the guidelines outlined in Principle #2. Messages should be packaged to the medium selected to communicate, whether it's Facebook, Twitter, Snapchat, Youtube, Instagram, LinkedIn, a blog, or online publication.

4. Assign a senior executive to champion the plan. The champion can't be just anyone. The champion needs to be actively engaged and recognized as a leader. He or she needs to be a Trust Leader who is customer-focused and SOCIAL (Sincere, Open,

Collaborative, Interested, Authentic and Likeable).

5. Involve all employees. Everybody has a part to play in building trust online. Employees from every part of the organization must support the online strategy. People want to hear from their peers online, from the people who are doing the job and from the subject matter experts. As Richard Eldelman told me, "It is no longer the CEO people want to hear from." Everyone can build relationships with social media influencers, as well as those stakeholders who are readers, engagers and even lurkers.

6. Publish simple, clear guidelines and train employees. Make it easy for employees to participate and contribute online. The online guide should be one straightforward page. It needs to cover the basics, steward employees and emphasize the business uses and objectives. The guidelines should recognize that personalization is necessary to foster trust and willingness for employees to share and connect. Provide training and show employees how to follow the guidelines.

7. Measure. Peter Drucker is famous for saying, "What gets measured gets managed." How are your social media efforts affecting your business objectives? For example, if one of your objectives is to deepen customer relationships of trust, what is the Client Trust Index™ score? Is it to generate leads and interest? How many leads and inquiries are there as a result of the activity? Analytical information is also useful to make informed decisions about performance.

8. Commit to making it happen. Strategy in business isn't worth anything until it is executed. It is about consistently doing what you say you are going to do. Building trust online takes time. You can't do it for a month and then forget about it for five months and expect the relationship will be the same five months later.

Here are a few more practical tips to build and strengthen trust online:

- Recommendations, third party testimonials and endorsements add credibility and social capital to individuals and companies. Recommendations from customers, partners and industry leaders are key components to your organization's profile.
- "Likes" enable a transference of trust as they can be viewed as endorsements.
- A picture says a thousand words. Post real, professional photos. If you are going to post photos of yourself, make sure they are authentic, not Photo shopped or depicting someone else. How is your profile affecting your (or your company's) brand?
- Videos can quickly explain complex concepts and can be the next best thing to face-to-face contact.
- Be accessible. If you point people to your website or to a landing page, make sure it is accessible and easy to use. We trust when we understand, when things are easy and accessible. When something is complicated we tend to distrust.
- Participate in groups. Listen and watch what questions and issues are important to your customers, and offer comments so people can get

familiar with you and get to know you.

- Post valuable content that is acting in the customer's best interest.

On the other side of the coin, expect problems when a social media policy is not in place or polices are not followed. One of the most notorious cases occurred when HMV record stores laid off employees in 2011, leaving one person, community manager Poppy Rose Cleere, in charge of the corporate Twitter account. Followers got a blow-by-blow account of the mass re-structuring through posts like "We're tweeting live from HR where we're all being fired! Exciting!" In just 20 minutes HMV's followers leapt from 61,500 to 73,350. But not for the right reasons.

Consider your online presence and ask yourself these key questions:

1. Are you presenting an authentic picture of your product, your company and yourself?
2. Is your social media presence all about you and your product? Are you focused on your customer?
3. Are you acting in the customer's best interests or your own best interests? Are you adding value and gaining followers by including them?
4. What are you contributing to the conversation? Do people engage you on social media or just passively watch and listen?
5. Are you achieving your objectives?

CASE STUDY

eBay's
Trust Model in the Online World

eBay is a customer-focused company that has earned trust online with its sellers and buyers since its inception in 1995. The company is a trust culture success story. As described in its LinkedIn profile, eBay "is where the world goes to shop, sell, and give." In 2016, Forbes listed eBay as one of the World's Most Valuable Brands.

I had the opportunity to meet Brian Bieron, executive director of global public policy at eBay. We sat on a panel together at the Symposium on ASIA-USA Partnership Opportunities conference in Atlanta, Georgia.

We discussed eBay's brand and the impact of the sellers and buyers' trust to its global export platform. He emphasized trust as a core value to eBay. "With internet enabled commerce, trust is a central and obvious need," he said. "Because everything is remote, the interactions are different. eBay is a platform model of global trade that allows sellers to establish some trust, and build relationships with people in other countries."

He made a number of points relating to the importance of trust: "Our founder, Pierre Omidyar, had the vision of eBay in the 90s as a remote, online small business entrepreneurial marketplace. Pierre said, 'People are basically good.' This is at the heart of the eBay model. People have to be able to trust the people they are doing business with. We work hard, enable and enforce standards that enforce trust."

CASE STUDY

eBay is based on a unique founding concept; at the time it was created it was an entirely new model for individuals and businesses.

"From the earliest days, how could we trust that someone sends a cheque, or the book or jewelry or the item will be shipped?" said Brian. "Trust was always part of founding principles and values." Users have to trust each other.

eBay enables its sellers to deliver on their promises.

"They are not in the same city or same country, they have to trust that they are going to engage in a trustworthy transaction," said Brian. "You can lose trust with a customer in one bad transaction. Shipping is so important; it is critical that the item gets there when the seller says it will. If it shows up late, it undermines trust. If we are doing our job well we are transferring a trust value to our users. We have customer guarantees because we want buyers to be happy."

I asked Brian how they protect the trust they have with their buyers and sellers. He said trusted sellers are key to the system working well.

eBay has a seller rating system, where customers rate the product and the experience. Their trust and safety division is continually reviewing buyer feedback to see if any buyers are complaining. The technology is set up through algorithms so the most visible items are those sold by people who sell good products and consistently deliver a good customer experience. "Buyers rate sellers. We are about buyers and sellers being happy."

At eBay, they want the customer experience and rating to be as good as the one they receive from the best retailers. We

CASE STUDY

also discussed critical trust risk points in an online business, including:

1. People listing things for sale that do not exist, or the description or photograph is not accurate. Regular businesses don't have this challenge. "When face to face, a buyer knows that a Tiffany set of dessert plates is real or not. They can compare the quality and the thickness of a real plate next to the one being sold," explained Brian.

2. Shipping and logistics.

3. Trustworthy sellers. eBay plays an intermediary role between good buyers and good sellers, fulfilling the terms of the buying agreement.

eBay creates trust with its buyers and sellers by applying the principles of trust and by insisting on accountability, transparency and delivering on its promises.

The days of intention-based marketing are over.
It is all about relationships.
Information flow cannot be controlled online.
The participatory nature of social media
promotes trust or distrust.

8

Communicating Trust to
Public Audiences: This is Not PR

In the current digital environment, almost every organization faces greater
scrutiny from a more informed and critical public, and an increasingly aggressive and intrusive media. This scrutiny can undermine an organization's reputation and ability to function effectively, or it can enhance its credibility and public
support. The challenge is to respond to this public environment in a manner that
builds trust instead of undermining it. The traditional 'public relations' approach of
most organizations does not meet this challenge effectively. Only a more proactive
strategy to communicating the organization's public messages will succeed.

THE ACTIVE APPROACH

One of the most significant trends in this second decade of the twenty-first century
is our growing insistence on more accountability from the organizations that affect
our lives. Simply put, we have become more critical, suspicious, and intolerant
of organizations and their leaders. As citizens, taxpayers, customers, employees
and shareholders, we want more information and better explanations. We want
transparency. Symptoms of public distrust are the proliferation of special interest
groups, greater demands for 'stakeholder input', and high numbers of consumer
complaints and lawsuits. This transformation has taken place in less than a single
generation and has been tracked by countless public opinion polls.

Many attribute this shift in the public mood to increased education levels, access to the Internet, the proliferation of user driven content, insecurity fostered by the pace of change, social media, and the inability of organizations to respond effectively to these changes with policies that build trust. Ronald Inglehart, author of Culture Shift in Advanced Industrial Society, uses the term "post materialism" to describe "the rise of a 'new class' in Western society, a stratum of highly educated and well paid young technocrats who take an adversary stance toward their society."

Lawrence Susskind and Patrick Field, authors of Dealing With An Angry Public, argue that business and government leaders "have fueled a rising tide of public distrust of both business and government;" the public has become more aware than ever that they "have covered up mistakes, concealed evidence of potential risks, made misleading statements, and often lied."

In 2017, The Edelman Trust Barometer reported that trust in business was at 55 per cent, which is lower than the historical average. Contemporary journalism fosters as well as reflects this public distrust by putting the spotlight on organizations and their leaders to an unprecedented degree. Everything has become the public's business. The Internet in particular has dramatically expanded our awareness of the issues and organizations influencing our lives. Also, there has been a significant change in the culture of popular journalism.

Intensified competition between news outlets is pressuring journalists to create more marketable news products in order to expand their audiences. Journalists have moved beyond simply reporting what has happened to 'uncovering' news stories, 'creating issues,' and 'packaging news products.' In the process, they have blurred the line between news and entertainment and given rise to the term 'infotainment.' indeed, some TV news producers now poll public opinion to discover which news stories will appeal to the largest audience.

Because good news if often boring and bad news sells, ambitious journalists strive to make their news stories provocative and controversial; to focus on critics' assertions and reactions; to highlight conflicts and problems; and to create contexts that dramatize quotes, events, and issues. Contemporary journalism strips away privacy and, with it, respect for institutions and those in authority. It personalizes, sensationalizes, and often oversimplifies the issues. While invoking 'the public's right to know,' journalists too often simply give the public what they think it wants.

> Journalists, better educated than their predecessors, are not intimidated by institutions or authorities. They are motivated to investigate, uncover, provoke, and focus on the negative, on mistakes, and on what is controversial: they draw a disproportionate amount of their information and quotes from critics and special-interest groups.

Only a few executives have begun to come to terms with this changing reality. Although the public and journalists are demanding greater transparency and putting more organizations in the public spotlight than ever, most executives continue to practice *ad hoc* and reactive public communications instead of building a culture of trust in their organizations.

THE AD HOC –
REACTIVE PUBLIC COMMUNICATIONS MODEL

With rare exceptions, corporate and government public relations and communications departments focus on hard news announcements and special events such as openings, anniversaries, new product launches, expansions, new initiatives and executive appointments. Otherwise, they pursue an *ad hoc* or reactive policy, letting journalists and others decide which messages the public gets about these organizations.

Executives who follow this model of public communication usually respond to public criticism or a negative news story about their organization by 'turning the other cheek' or by 'keeping their head down' so as not to 'feed the press,' hoping it will all blow away in a couple of days. As one executive rationalized, 'the spouting whale gets the harpoon.'

THE AD HOC –
REACTIVE PUBLIC COMMUNICATIONS POLICY

- Does not have a communications objective process on building trust.
- Ignores public misperceptions and criticism.
- Unnecessarily limits information about the organization's decisions and plans.
- Communicates to the public only when pressured to do so or on an ad hoc basis with sporadic hard news announcements and advertisements.

This traditional public relations approach is increasingly ineffective in the digital environment in which aggressive journalists, special interest groups, and critics compete with each other to determine which messages the public gets about the organization, and all too often those messages undermine the public's trust in the organization.

Active Public Communications

To build trust in the digital environment, organizations must move beyond simply communicating to the public on an ad hoc and reactive basis. They must set and aggressively manage their own public communications agenda by practicing proactive public communications.

Proactive public communications begins with the organization's commitment to:

- Behaving with integrity and striving to operate in harmony with the public interest
- Listening to public concerns and addressing them
- Correcting its behaviour when it discovers it is doing the wrong thing

Proactive public communications is built on three pillars: a transparent organization, clear public communications objectives and a plan for achieving them, and a commitment to aggressively managing the media relations function on a daily basis.

Proactive Public Communications

- Strives to make the organization's policies, plans, and activities as transparent as possible.
- Determines the messages its public will get about the organization, and develops a plan to communicate those messages.
- Manages its public communications media function aggressively by anticipating and responding to news stories, events and issues that relate to the organization and its communication's objectives.

THE TRANSPARENT ORGANIZATION

Most organizations are gratuitously secretive. They needlessly withhold information, informing the public and, indeed, often their own employees on 'a need to know' basis only. Obviously, every organization must maintain the confidentiality of certain information related to competitive, legal, personnel, and customer issues. Subject to such qualifications, an effective public communications policy begins with management's acceptance of the radical notion that the more the public knows about the organization's plans, challenges, ad activities, the better.

As we have discussed, transparency fosters trust, credibility, and empathy. When an organization keeps the public well informed, it is rewarded with a public that judges it more fairly and with more empathy. Secretive organizations have the opposite effect.

Secrecy, more than anything else, undermines credibility, promotes misunderstanding, and generates suspicion. Its effect is to make the organization vulnerable to unfounded rumours and to unwanted exposure by investigative journalists anxious to uncover 'the real story.' "Tell us something we didn't already know!" is a common command from editors; which is to say most negative news stories focus on the information vacuums, the surprising disclosures, the unexplained policies and motives, and 'the secrets' of corporate or government entities. Simply put, lack of information from the organization leads journalists and the public to assume the information is being withheld intentionally.

Transparency has another benefit: The more the public knows about the organization, the more difficult it is for a single incident or negative news story to significantly affect the public's trust. A public that is well informed about the organization can put the single news story into perspective.

On the other hand, while transparency puts negative news into a broad context, the lack of transparency magnifies the significance of negative news. If the only news the public has heard about the organization is negative, that is what will stick.

Proactive communications managers tell the public and journalists everything they want to know about the organization unless there is a good reason not to do so. These managers know that trust, understanding, and sympathy are fostered when the public is well informed.

COMMUNICATIONS OBJECTIVES AND PLAN

Along with being as transparent as possible about their organizations, proactive public communicators set specific objectives and have a plan for achieving them that they continually adapt to the changing news environment.

Effective Communications Objectives:

- Advance the overall corporate goals of the organization including building a strong brand of trustworthiness.
- Address what the audience does not know or misunderstands.
- Are achievable within a limited time, usually within one or two years or less.

One way to establish communications objectives is to answer the following questions:

- Which message or messages, if communicated to the public, would have the biggest positive impact on the organization's effectiveness and reputation?
- Which two or three characteristics do you want the public to attribute to the organization that it currently does not?
- What is the reputation of the organization now and what would you like it to be in two years?
- What misconceptions does the public have about the organization that, if corrected, would enable it to more easily achieve its goals?
- What do you want the public to know about the organization that is currently does not know?
- What issues must the organization address to protect or advance its interests?

Along with these questions, the following points must be taken into account:

- The policies and actions of the organization must support its public messages or they will lack credibility. Indeed sometimes the most important message can be a "demonstration message." What is does must support what it says. For example

  1. unethical behaviour resulted in the dismissal of one of more employees.
  2. the removal of a flawed product from distribution.

3. admission of wrong behavior or a bad practice accompanied by steps to ensure it is not repeated.

+   Communications objectives should be targeted to specific audiences: employees, customers, shareholders, or the public.

+   Communications objectives must support the organization's corporate goals. That is their only purpose.

With clear communications objectives, the organization can develop a plan for achieving them. The next step is to create the messages that will achieve the desired outcomes with the targeted audiences. Then comes the task of determining the tactics, activities, and tools required to communicate these messages. These may include such things as: advertisements, direct mailings, news releases, news conferences, speaking engagements, and media interviews.

PROACTIVE TRUST - BUILDING POLICIES

Communications managers have a challenge that extends beyond being transparent and implementing the organization's communications plan. They must proactively manage their public communications agenda every day.

Their challenge is to:

+   Cultivate positive working relationships with the journalists, bloggers, and stakeholders who have the potential to report on the organization and the issues related to it.
+   Work with colleagues to manage their online brand and experience.

- Inform the public about the organization's activities, and initiatives on a timely basis.
- Monitor and aggressively respond to news events, criticisms, misperceptions and manage stories related to the organization.
- Pre-empt criticism and concerns about the organization's policies and activities and values by publicly addressing them before critics do;
- Develop communications response plans to deal with negative news stories and events than can be anticipated;
- Condition public opinion to expect and accept changes in the organization's activities and policies and the possibility of negative news developments long before they occur.
- Avoid surprising the public, it is rarely welcomed. Give customers lots of notice.

IMPLEMENTING A PROACTIVE COMMUNICATIONS POLICY

Traditional public relations practitioners and senior executives must transform their thinking if they are to move from being reactive to proactive, from withholding information to being transparent. They must manage the news and information the public gets about the organization instead of letting journalists and others do it for them.

To succeed, a proactive trust building communications policy must have the full support of the organization's top management team. It must become an integral part of the organization's corporate culture.

Senior management must be fully committed to implementing a proactive public communications policy. This is not an easy task. Becoming more transparent and proactively communicating with journalists and the public are difficult challenges for most executives.

A proactive trust building communications policy brings with it risks, particularly when it is introduced in a traditional public relations environment. Executives suddenly empowered to speak to journalists might say 'the wrong thing,' or say what someone else should have said, or could have said better. Employees empowered to manage social media must communicate messages, values and policies. Furthermore, when an organization becomes transparent, it will inevitably reveal some warts.

A proactive public communications policy will never fully control the messages the public gets about the organization. Journalists will still have their own agendas, and, in spite of their best efforts, executives will sometimes be taken out of context or misquoted. Special interest groups and critics will still exist, but being proactive still beats being reactive every day of the week.

Proactive communications managers have difficult challenges in any organization. They are often blamed when the news is bad and ignored when the news is good. Some expect the public communications manager to cover up or at least explain in a positive way almost anything. Senior management must acknowledge that even the most competent communications manager cannot compensate for ineffective policies, stupidity, and blunders. If poor communications did not cause the problem, good communicators can't fix it.

Although effective communications may soften the public's reaction to an organization's behaviour, the fact is that the most important thing is the behaviour itself. As the saying goes, "What you do speaks so loudly that I cannot hear what you are saying."

9

Red Flags -
Identifying your Trust Risk Points

Sometimes it starts with finding out about a project your customer is working on without your involvement, or that the customer has another supplier for something your company could have handled. Other times it might be a lack of response, or a notification that your customer is 'trying out' a new provider or they are planning to issue a Request for Proposal (RFP) for the offerings you currently provide. Often it is the account manager who sees the signs first.

These red flags indicate that customers might be losing trust in your organization and it's time to pay close attention. With these signs come business problems including:

+ Declining revenues
+ Fewer sales
+ More complaints
+ Lack of repeat business, starting each quarter fresh
+ Customer retention is a problem
+ Longer sales cycles
+ Fewer customer referrals
+ Lost business
+ Fewer partnership opportunities

Rarely does it start with a complaint. Unfortunately, as we have noted, 96 per cent of unhappy customers do not complain and 91 per cent will simply leave and never come back, according to research from F1 Financial Training Services. Even worse, the Edelman Trust Barometer suggests nearly seven out of 10 unhappy customers criticize an organization or products they do not trust to friends.

Fortune Magazine's "100 best companies to work for" – in which trust comprises 60 per cent of the criteria – earned more than four times the returns of the broader marker over the prior seven years, according to the 2005 Russell Investment Report.

IDENTIFYING CRITICAL TRUST RISK POINTS

Remember trust is established and maintained through the sum of all the experiences an individual has with everyone in a company.

Critical trust points therefore are any interactions with an organization where trust can be gained or lost. Therefore, every separate interaction with your organization could be a critical trust point. Every organization or profession has specific risk points and trust issues. Examples include:

- Colleges must have faculty with the proper credentials, knowledge and experience to teach.
- Restaurants must offer food that is safe.
- Software companies must deliver on their promise that the software must function as advertised.
- Webhosting companies must be reliable and prevent any loss of Internet connections.
- Financial advisors must act in the customer's best interest; they must offer honest, credible services and advice.
- Associations and governing bodies must maintain the highest professional standards and ensure that members comply with the standards, ethics and

codes of conduct.

+ Regulators must act in the public interest.
+ Manufacturing companies must offer safe environments and produce safe, reliable products.
+ Professional services firms must offer honest advice and services and act in the best interest of their customer.

DEFINITION: CRITICAL TRUST RISK POINT

A critical trust risk point is any interaction that may cause injury or harm to an organization's trust. They often arise from experiences people have with an organization's experts, leaders and front line employees as well as products and services. Customer facing employees often present the most significant trust risk point for a company. Trust is assessed and reassessed continually through experiences with the organization and its critical trust risk points.

Some interactions pose significantly more risks to trust than others. Interactions are critical to the development or protection of a relationship of trust with your customer or partner. For example, trust can be lost or compromised when the CEO, technician or retail clerk submits a bill that doesn't add up or ring true to form.

A trust risk point is anything that undermines trust or confidence in your business or organization.

One way to discover your critical trust risk points is to think about and map out the full customer experience with your company; from first hearing about you to researching your business, to evaluating whether or not they will work with you, to the first contact and so on.

WHAT ARE THE TRUST VULNERABILITIES
IN YOUR ORGANIZATION?

Some individuals in a company pose high-risk points and others do not. The front line staff of any organization has a significant impact on creating trust with the organization. Other examples include executives who interact with customers or external stakeholders, sales professionals, business development staff, communications and public relations, investor and stakeholder relations professionals, customer service, customer support, project managers, supply chain managers, the marketing department, installers, consultants, professional services professionals and accounts receivable.

Any individual in contact with customers and/or external stakeholders on an ongoing basis must be particularly sensitive to the challenge of building and maintaining trust.

Every business is unique. It is important to sit down and identify your critical trust points and vulnerabilities. It could be the bus driver, retail clerk, sales person, investor or media relations officer, telephone attendant, bank teller, shelf stocker or data security officer, Where are your critical trust points and what are you doing about them? Those in contact with customers and external stakeholders are responsible for earning and protecting trust for the organization.

Ask yourself: What roles and functions consistently interact with customers and external partners in your organization? Be as specific as you can be.

In addition to interactions with people, critical trust points also include an interaction with a place, an event, a product or a service.

Examples of places may include offices or sites of business, manufacturing plants, websites, Facebook pages, LinkedIn pages, Twitter feed, Instagram, Snapchat and Pinterest sites right through to proposals, documents, emails, presentations and advertisements.

Ask yourself: what parts of your organization are customers, potential customers, potential students, funders, partners, suppliers and external stakeholders evaluating and deciding to trust?

Examples of events may include open houses, conferences and annual meetings, trade shows, ceremonies, customer or stakeholder visits, tours, trials, and receptions.

Ask yourself: What are the events that your organization hosts, attends or participates in that customers, partners, suppliers and external stakeholders evaluate whether or not to trust your organization, your team and your colleagues?

Other issues organizations must consider include regulatory, certification and licensing, to name just a few.

COMMON CRITICAL TRUST RISK POINTS

Front Line Employees

- Rude or disrespectful employees
- Arguing with customers
- Failure to admit mistakes
- Incompetent or uninformed staff
- Breaking a confidence
- Missing shipping and delivery deadlines
- Mismanaging project or deadline expectations
- Unethical behavior
- Poor or inaccurate advice
- Getting customer's name wrong
- Inaccurate diagnosis of problems
- Lack of respect for customer's opinion
- Attitude of the front line employees
- Inappropriate social media activity by employees
- Failure to supervise inexperienced or junior employees
- Misleading customers about the product, the scope of project price or purchase agreements.
- Confidential customer data being leaked
- Employee media interviews
- Mismanaging price or scope of work expectations
- Employees cheating on expense accounts

COMMON CRITICAL TRUST RISK POINTS

Product, Services and Policies

- Cyber threats data/ IT / security/ confidentiality breaches of data or information
- Handling of returns, warranty, service issues
- Product safety or reliability concerns
- Misleading price expectations
- Missing shipping and delivery deadlines
- Mismanaging project or deadline expectations
- Allowing different pricing for different customers
- Poor installation of product or service
- Product flaws
- Product recalls
- Inaccurate diagnosis of problems
- Failure to meet service level agreements
- Confidential customer data being leaked
- Mismanaging price or scope of work expectations
- Incompetent or uninformed staff

COMMON CRITICAL TRUST RISK POINTS

Management Risk Points

- Arguing with customers
- Mismanaged events
- Failure to admit mistakes
- Incompetent or uninformed staff
- Breaking a confidence
- Conflicts of interest
- Missing shipping and delivery deadlines
- Mismanaging project or deadline expectations
- Unethical behavior
- Poor or inaccurate advice
- Getting customer's name wrong
- Failure to supervise inexperienced or junior employees
- Allowing different pricing for different customers
- Misleading customers about the product, the scope of project price or purchase agreements.
- Confidential customer data being leaked
- Lack of respect for customer's opinion
- CEO or Executive media interviews
- Inappropriate social media activity by employees
- Mismanaging price or scope of work expectations
- Employees cheating on expense accounts
- Cyber security breaches, intrusions and cyber attacks

Managing price expectations is important for every company and every industry. Trusted advisors manage expectations up front. Misleading means not telling you something. Unfortunately most of us can think of a time when we were misled about prices or fees. Several years ago I was working with an accounting firm. The accountant was preparing my taxes and my husband's.

I called the accountant to follow up on an item he was asking about. After I shared with him the information he was looking for it came up that I was planning to sell my workbooks, Building Trust with Customers: A Workbook, online. We discussed how to collect and account for the sales tax. This took about five minutes.

We then talked about his recent vacation, my children and a business event that was happening in our city. We talked for about forty minutes in total. Thirty days later I received a bill for $600. The description was 'telephone conversation (40 minutes) and research relating to selling workbooks online'.

As we discussed in principle number 4 – customers do not like surprises. I was caught off guard by the bill. It motivated me to stop calling. I did not realize that I would receive a bill for talking about his vacation and my children and answering a simple question about taxes. It destroyed the relationship. When I saw the bill I thought: "Why did he charge me for 35 minutes to chit-chat?" It felt like he was taking advantage of me. After three years of working with him, couldn't he answer one simple question? Why wouldn't he tell me that I was going to be charged for talking to him on the phone? Unfortunately, the accountant trained me to stop telephoning and stop talking to him. And he never called me. He emailed, but never called.

I didn't understand the scope of the typical accountant's business model as well as I do today.

The next year I asked him in an email how much the bill was going to be. After he completed the returns, we received an invoice in the mail. It was for $300 more than the original quote. Again I was taken aback. I did what the majority of the population does, I did not say anything to him, I did not complain. Like most unhappy customers, I left the firm and found a new accountant.

Everyone's critical trust risk points are different. It is important to get to know your customer. In the example, the accountant failed to take the time to understand his client. When I asked him to telephone me if he had questions, he would email me. He never returned my calls. He never reached out to review my financial statements with me; they were emailed to me. All of these little things were critical trust risk points. The most significant one was the bill. Twice I was unpleasantly surprised.

Managing customer expectations is critical. None of us like surprises. Make sure you let your customers know what the bill includes. Do you raise the issue of price before they do? Do your customers know the total cost of doing business with you?

Telltale signs that your employees may be undermining trust

- Employees do not fully understand the challenges your customer faces in purchasing your products and services
- You are not certain that your customers are satisfied with all members of the staff they encounter
- Your pricing policies are not clear and easy to understand
- You believe you may have lost customers because of staff mistakes
- You suspect you lost customers because of staff attitudes
- Not every staff member is fully informed about your product or service
- You miss deadlines with customers
- Customers complain about poor service or product quality
- Some employees do not adequately respect customer opinions
- Some employees are impatient with customers
- You lack customer feedback
- Employees are not strict about client confidentiality

In many cases these shortcomings are the result of poor supervision or company policy and practices, poor product quality and lack of focus on customer. The question has to be asked: is this a reflection on management's lack of commitment to building and protecting trust?

When companies undertake to determine their critical trust risk points, we often perform Trust Risk Point Audit. We identify their critical trust risk points; assign a rating of the risk: high, moderate or low on a scale of one to ten; identify the specific action required to address the risk; determine the time line and who is responsible for carrying out the task.

Key Questions to Ask:

1. What are the most crucial trust issues for your profession or organization?

2. How does the customer experience your organization?

3. Which positions represent the high-risk areas?

4. What are the events that your organization hosts, attends or participates in that customers, potential customers, potential students, funders, partners, suppliers and external stakeholders evaluate whether or not to trust your organization, your team and your colleagues?

10

When Trust Fails: Creating a Trust Crisis Response Strategy

Communicating with integrity builds and protects trust. It also helps on the path of restoring trust when it has been damaged. Behaving with integrity and striving to do what is in the public or the customers' best interest is top priority while following these guidelines.

Before you communicate you have to do the right thing or fix what you are doing wrong. Nothing is more powerful than doing the right thing. As we have mentioned, "Actions speak louder than words."

Follow these guidelines when dealing with a crisis or a trust issue:

1. *Acknowledge there is a problem or an issue when there is one. Do this in a timely manner.*

   Do not deny there is a problem when you know one exists. Examples of such denials include statements like: "This will not affect your product or our service offering," "We are looking into it to see if there is a problem," "We are looking into it," "No comment, our lawyer has advised us not to talk about this right now."

2. *Keep employees as fully informed as possible. Employees should be the first to know when and if there is a problem, what has happened, and how the company is going to respond.*

   Do not keep the employees in the dark. Tell them forthrightly what is going on. Examples of what NOT to say: "We have time to get a strategy before the public finds out," "The less employees know the better before we figure out what to do," "Make sure managers keep their mouths shut about this until we have to tell them," "Employees may post on social media, don't tell them yet."

3. *Be honest and transparent with your stakeholders about any problematic situations. Inform your most important stakeholders first. Tailor the message to each stakeholder group as it relates to them.*
   Do not be secretive about what is happening. Examples of being secretive include statements like: "We don't know any more about this than you do at this point," or "As far as we know this situation is under control," or "We are still in the dark about what it really happening here."

4. *Accept responsibility.*
   Do not refuse to accept corporate responsibility. Do not finger point or blame a group of employees, supplier or third party. Examples: "This is not how our company does business," "No law has been broken here," "A few people made some mistakes and we are looking into it," "This is our supplier's product that malfunctioned, not ours," "Our supplier is at fault, not us."

5. *Be specific about what steps you are taking to address the problem, resolve the issue or correct the mistake. The plan should include specific actions and timelines.*
   Do not be vague about what you are doing to try to fix a problem. Do not make statements that communicate a lack of urgency or give the problem a low priority. Examples: "We are going to form a task force to look at this," "This is complicated and it is going to take us some time to fully understand the situation," "We are going to consult with the affected parties."

6. *Act with urgency. Communicate the importance of the priority placed on the issue. Be as specific as you can be with timelines and plans.*

Do not delay unnecessarily before you act and communicate. Do not use stalling tactics. Examples of stalling: "We are going to take this under advisement and assess the situation," "We are going to consult with our lawyers," "We are still trying to understand what is going on," "We are waiting to hear what might happen next before we do anything," "We do not want to get ahead of ourselves until we get all the facts."

7. *Acknowledge the impact of the mistake or the issue as it relates to your employees, customers, the organization, industries and communities it affects.*

Do not trivialize negative impacts of mistakes or leave out any important stakeholder group. Examples: "This will not affect many people," "Do not panic," "Do not read too much into this situation until we find out what is really going on," "This is a common problem we are used to dealing with."

8. *Realistically estimate the magnitude of correcting the mistake or issue. If it will take weeks, months or years, affect a lot of people or cost money, say so.*

Do not underestimate or minimize the challenge of correcting the mistake. Examples: "We have this fully under control," "This is a small issue, we will have it fixed soon," "Do not be concerned, it will be contained soon," "People shouldn't make a mountain out of a molehill," "We don't have to use a sledge hammer to kill a fly."

9. *Listen, acknowledge and address stakeholders concerns. Seek their feedback and questions so you understand their concerns and fully acknowledge their seriousness.*

Do not ignore or fail to listen to or address public, customer or stakeholder concerns. Examples: "I think they are misinformed about this," "The media doesn't understand our situation,""This is too complicated to explain in simple terms,""This is an easy fix, don't worry."

10.   *Acknowledge and correct any and all misperceptions and misinformation about a problem.*

Do not ignore misperceptions and misinformation. If you do, people will connect their own dots and will think the worst. Examples: "That is not the real concern people should have,""This kind of accident doesn't happen very often,""Our record is better than our competitors on this matter,""We are not going to respond to all of the rumors about this,""This is an industry problem not just ours."

11.   *Plan for a crisis. The plan should include: the list of critical trust risk points in your organization; a prioritized list of stakeholder; key messages for each stakeholder and how you will communicate with them. The plan should also identify your spokespeople and ways to monitor the success of the plan.*

Do not assume you will never face a crisis. Do not ignore your organization's critical trust risk points. Examples: "We are not going to cross that bridge unless we have to,""Let's just stay out of the target zone,""We will deal with that if and when it happens."

Nothing is more powerful than doing the right thing.

CASE STUDY

Regaining Trust After a Crisis
Maple Leaf Foods

Breaking trust can damage, even destroy an organization's viability, credibility and reputation.

As we saw in the Prologue, in 2008 an outbreak of listeriosis caused the Canadian Food Inspection Agency to issue a "health hazard" alert for Maple Leaf Foods, prompting the company to recall more than 200 products. It became one the worst cases of food contamination in Canadian history, killing 22 people and making thousands ill. Food and health security became a critical trust issue for Maple Leaf Foods. The company had no choice but to earn back the trust of its customers.

This case describes how Maple Leaf Foods regained public trust after the listeria outbreak in 2008. Specifically, the media's coverage to the responses and the actions the company took to restore and nurture the public's trust.

Maple Leaf is one of Canada's largest food processors with approximately $3.3 billion CAD in annual sales for fiscal year 2016. Headquartered in Toronto, Canada, the company exports to over 80 countries, has 120 plants, and employs 19,500 employees in Canada, the United States, Mexico, the United Kingdom and Asia.

CASE STUDY

The Situation: Outbreak of Listeria and Deaths caused by Maple Leaf Foods Products

On August 16, 2008, an outbreak of listeria caused the Canadian Food Inspection Agency to issue a "health hazard" alert on Maple Leaf products. Listeria was traced back to the Sure Slice Roast Beef product from Maple Leaf's Bartor Road facility in Toronto.

On August 17, the company voluntarily recalled its Sure Slice product. Within the next three days, health officials announced one death and stated that 16 cases of listeria were linked to the outbreak. Maple Leaf announced that it was expanding its recall to an additional 20 products.

On August 23, one week later, tests by the Canadian Food Inspection Agency confirmed the link between a food-borne illness, caused by a bacterium listeria moncytogenes and meat products from the Maple Leaf plant. As a precaution, Maple Leaf expanded its recall to include all 220 products produced at the Bartor Road facility. From August 23, 2008 to October 1, 2009 announcements of new cases of listeria, deaths, test findings and events continued to surface and add to the crisis. These events can be described as access points of trust or distrust. Each event was reported in the media. The events ranged in severity from: deaths, to the prime minister of Canada ordering an investigation, to involvement from the provincial agriculture ministers, plant closures, lawsuits, hiring freezes, to loss of revenue.

This listeria outbreak became one the worst cases of food contamination in Canadian history, killing 22 people, and making thousands of people ill. It also became the biggest crisis in the company's history. The company's trust was on the line.

CASE STUDY

Without trust in the safety of the products, consumers may cease to purchase, revenues will decline, shareholders will lose confidence, causing a share price decline, inspection agencies will question the operation of facilities, and distributors may reconsider their relationship with the company.

The Significant Role of the Media during a Crisis: setting the agenda and the tone

For nearly 100 years, scholars have believed that the news media plays a major role in influencing stakeholder's opinions. Media has the ability to alter perceptions and tell the story in a 'matter of fact style' resulting in the priorities of the media strongly influencing the priorities of the public and the company's stakeholders.

Since the first study in 1968 by Max McCombs of the University of Texas and Donald Shaw of University of North Carolina, more than 300 published empirical studies demonstrate that the news affects stakeholders' opinions. In 1988, a poll in Indiana showed evidence of significant relationships between media exposure, issue salience and the effects on an audience's knowledge, opinions and observable behaviour. A study conducted at Oxford University in 2005 concluded that during a crisis, the media set the agenda and tone. Ninety per cent of the communication was controlled by the media, not by the organization.

According to the internationally recognized agenda setting role of mass communications authority Professor Max McCombs of The University of Texas, media influence goes "beyond attitudes and opinions, the pictures of reality created by the mass media have implications for personal behaviours". Furthermore, the reality created by the media affects not only attitude, opinion and

CASE STUDY

behaviour, it affects a stakeholder's trust in an organization. Trust is usually tested and can become a critical issue during a crisis if it is not proactively managed.

Stakeholders look to and evaluate access points during a crisis: how do they communicate, behave and serve during a crisis?

Maple Leaf stakeholders included: consumers, including individuals in jurisdictions where products were distributed and potentially consumed; Canadian food safety regulatory bodies; financial regulators; government officials; distributors, including retail and restaurant distributors; investors; suppliers; shareholders and the investment community; media; communities across Canada, including Toronto and the 19 other communities where plants reside; industry associations; the legal community; provinces where cases of listeria were reported; competitors and similar type companies in the food processing industry; and customers, consumers and regulators of Maple Leaf Foods Bread Division, Canada Bread. The stakeholders all had varying interests in the food contamination crisis.

During the crisis, external stakeholders develop trust in the organization through various 'access points' or customer touch points such as an interaction with the CEO through the media, or the telephone hotline representative. These touch points and individuals bring the organization to life. Other access points for Maple Leaf included: spokespersons, sales account managers, the Chief Health and Safety Officer, the website, YouTube, investor and media relations' officers.

When there's trouble or even doubt about a company or organization, stakeholders quickly look for a consistent, credible source

CASE STUDY

of information. During a crisis we want to hear from the leader, from the person who is ultimately responsible. We want people and leaders to be accountable. Confidence in leaders increases when they take responsibility. At Maple Leaf, CEO Michael McCain took the role of primary spokesperson. Choosing the CEO as the primary spokesperson builds trust in that individual as a leader inside and outside the company.

Clear Goal: Restoring Trust started with the CEO taking responsibility and an empathetic, sincere apology

Effective media relations are a critical action to restore and maintain trust during a crisis. It's pretty cleaar that the media coverage and the company's handling of it played a major role in restoring the public's trust.

McCain's statements were consistent, reliable and committed the company to the steps it would take to regain the customer's trust.

Maple Leaf's goal was clear: to restore trust. According to company executive Charlie Scott, during the crisis, restoring the public's trust through strong, fact based, open and transparent communication became the company's number one priority.

The Apology: Timely, Sincere, empathetic, compassionate, accountable and courageous

Within hours of learning of the outbreak Michael McCain publicly acknowledged it, apologized, and took responsibility for the disaster and offered sympathy to everyone affected. This was delivered

CASE STUDY

on television and YouTube to reach the greatest number of people.

"When listeria was discovered in the product, we launched immediate recalls to get it off the shelf, then we shut the plant down. Tragically our products have been linked to illness and loss of life. To Canadians who are ill and to the families who have lost loved ones, I offer my deepest sympathies. Words cannot begin to express our sadness for your pain...But this week, our best efforts failed and we are deeply sorry. This is the toughest situation we have faced in 100 years as a company. We know this has shaken your confidence in us; I commit to you that our actions are guided by putting your interests first,"

– Michael McCain, CEO, Maple Leaf Foods, Saturday, August 23, 2008

The initial apology was sincere and demonstrated compassion as the CEO expressed sympathy and stated that the interests of Canadians would be put before the company's interest.

Many in the media, including bloggers, academics and industry insiders remarked that the apology was candid. The Guardian called it "abject" and Dana Flavelle of The Toronto Star noted that "unlike most CEO's, the President and CEO, Michael McCain accepted responsibility."

An opinion piece in the Toronto Star written by Douglas Powell described the statement as "powerful and compelling." The Guardian reported nearly six months after the apology that the response "showed both genuine compassion and cutthroat business sense" and that "his apology could not have seemed more personal or heartfelt." The apology expressed empathy, compassion and sincerity, allowing stakeholders to begin re-

CASE STUDY

storing trust in Maple Leaf Foods.

Several media outlets remarked how McCain accepted responsibility. The Toronto Star reported that "It takes courage to take responsibility ... McCain showed admirable resolve when he stepped forward this week to address the public's desire for accountability." The repeated coverage of McCain cemented into the minds of the public that the CEO was taking responsibility and he became the access point of trust during the event.

Open, transparent and sharing plans

Openness is a key behaviour that restores trust. We recognize sincere, genuine openness. Sincerity is a key characteristic. The Globe and Mail implied McCain's sincerity through the narrative. "The TV spot felt artless and genuine, right from the declaration of culpability to the un-slick presence of Michael McCain in his open-collar shirt."

Studies demonstrate that willingness to trust leadership figures depends on how open those leaders are with relevant information. Janet Davison of CBC News, wrote "the company's CEO did something few others facing a similar crisis had ever done.... he told consumers what the company was doing."

In 1991, John Butler, of Clemson University conducted an empirical study that supported 'openness' as one of several conditions of trust. Openness is especially important when competence is low. McCain's openness and honesty in disclosing that his team knew the root cause of the listeria helped win back customer trust. By remaining transparent and using frequent communication to share any new information will contribute to

CASE STUDY

rebuilding the trust that may have been lost.

Built on a Foundation of Values and Doing the Right Thing

Throughout the crisis, Maple Leaf mentioned its values many times. "We have a highly principled set of values in our company, and they guided us throughout, including putting customers first and being clear and accepting responsibility". One might argue that company values became universal standards and guidelines to answer moral questions. Among those values is 'Do what is right'.

'Doing the right thing' became a key message and central component of the Company's PR strategy. As stated by Michael McCain, "(We) tried to figure out the right thing to do in the middle of this terrible situation". Throughout the campaign, Maple Leaf provided clear, consistent messages, delivered primary by one spokesperson, the CEO.

When I asked Chief Operations Officer Scott McCain about the decision he said, "It was straightforward, we wanted to do the right thing for our customers, our employees, and for the public."

Doing the Right Thing and Acting in the Public's Best Interest

Subsequent actions and messages delivered by Maple Leaf illustrate that decisions were made based on doing the right thing and acting in the public's best interest. One example of this is the

CASE STUDY

following statement made by the CEO:

> *"Going through the crisis, there are two advisors I've paid no attention to. The first are the lawyers and the second are the accountants. It's not about the money or the legal liability – this is about being accountable for providing consumers with safe food."*

The communications strategy employed during the crisis was built on "demonstrating the highest level of responsibility possible" according to Maple Leaf's Vice President of Communications, Jeanette Jones.

Jones cites four tenets to this approach:
1. Take responsibility
2. Put public health and consumer interests first
3. Lead in open and factual communication
4. Implement a decisive action plan

These tenets support the principles of trust. Taking responsibility, demonstrating commitment to the long term, acting in the public's best interest and putting public health and consumer interests first. Commit to always doing the right thing. When a mistake is made, fix it. Be honest and transparent and communicate using clear, concrete language.

    Maple Leaf's decision to close the plant demonstrates the principle of doing the right thing and acting the public's best interest, not in the company's short-term financial interests. The closure inflicted considerable pain on the plant workers,

CASE STUDY

who lost their jobs and on the company and its investors. Profits dropped because of the lost production. The benefits of closing the plant included stopping the spread of listeria and improving public safety. Maple Leaf was applauded for this decision. McCain was widely praised for promptly recalling the products from the Toronto plant, even if those not linked to listeria in any way.

Following the plant closure and the initial apology, Maple Leaf employed a variety of media for public outreach including: five press conferences, media plant tours, television advertisements that were later posted to YouTube, full page newspaper advertisements, investor conference calls, a telephone hot line, a food safety microsite and the Maple Leaf website. Employing multiple media demonstrated an effort to provide the greatest number of individuals with equal access to the messages. It is important to note that other than YouTube and the website, Maple Leaf Foods did not have a social media presence. The Company joined Facebook in December of 2010 and Twitter in August of 2011.

Familiarity can breed and restore trust

Familiarity through repeated interaction and direct interpersonal contact leads to trust. The media coverage of Maple Leaf was consistent and the communication from Maple Leaf Foods to its external publics was frequent. Consistent and frequent communication builds and strengthens trust. In addition to traditional media, the public was looking at the website for information. As reported by Christine Adams in PR in Canada, there were 363,000 website hits for 'Maple Leaf' and 'Maple Leaf + Listeria'

CASE STUDY

in the first month of the crisis.

When a third party credible source speaks well of a company the trust associated with the third party can be transferred to the organization, especially for people with no relationship with the organization. This gives people a term of reference with the company. This can be extremely effective when rebuilding trust.

As a result of his frank approach to dealing with the listeria crisis, McCain was chosen Business Newsmaker of the Year in 2008 in an annual survey of editors and broadcasters by The Canadian Press. The coverage used positive language. "That public health disaster turned business success story has made the Maple Leaf CEO Canada's 2008 Business Newsmaker of the Year."

Consistent, predictable and reliable behaviour rebuilds trust. Inconsistencies between words, behaviours and actions diminish trust. Actions speak louder than words. The media consistently reported on the actions, reliability, predictability and good judgment of the company. For example, the CBC reported, "A day later, Maple Leaf upgraded a precautionary recall of 23 of its products...to all 220 packaged meats from the plant, which has been shut down."

Several articles were published comparing Maple Leaf to companies in similar situations. For example, five days after the link between the listeria outbreak and Maple Leaf was confirmed, CBC News published an article titled How Maple Leaf Foods is handling the Listeria Outbreak. It commented on how McCain personally took ownership, "if you look at the Maple Leaf example, we saw a lot more openness and transparency and really a lot of leadership." Taking ownership and being accountable builds trust. Accountability and ownership

CASE STUDY

demonstrate capabilities and ethical behaviour and are part of delivering on a promise. When comparing Maple Leaf to other organizations, the media consistently described Maple Leaf and McCain in favourable language.

Commitment to the long term

One strategy Maple Leaf employed that supported the principle of commitment to the long term was to create a forum on food safety issues. Maple Leaf created a 'food safety consortium' to grow grass root support from the food industry, while showing responsibility and leadership. Members included Maple Leaf employees, wholesale customers, inspectors, government officials, distributors, health commissions, companies in similar food processing industries and competitors to Maple Leaf.

The objective of the consortium was to provide food safety education and support to the entire industry. This activity is directly in line with the principles of involving and engaging in discussion, demonstrating commitment to the long term and showing they are acting in the public's best interest.

People trust individuals and by extension, organizations that they believe have good intentions and motivations. The Globe and Mail reported on McCain's demonstration of compassion, recognition of fault and immediate acceptance of responsibility by directly quoting him: "(We) tried to figure out the right thing to do in the middle of this terrible situation," "We have a highly principled set of values in our company, and they guided us throughout, including putting customers first and being clear and accepting responsibility."

CASE STUDY

Positive comparisons instill confidence and trust

Several articles from CBC compared Maple Leaf's response to Johnson and Johnson's response handling of the tampered Tylenol packaging crisis in 1982. Johnson and Johnson's handing of the crisis is still hailed as a textbook case of how to handle a crisis. Within one year Tylenol regained its market share. In 2008 Johnson and Johnson was named one of the world's most trusted companies. Johnson and Johnson is still considered one of the most trusted companies in the world, earning a place on Forbes Magazine's regular list of global trusted brands.

Comparing Maple Leaf Foods to Johnson and Johnson transfers trust to Maple Leaf. Often when companies have a crisis they arrange to have third party credible spokespeople endorse the company or discuss the situation publicly. An endorsement from a highly credible, trusted individual from another company can strengthen trust.

The case of Maple Leaf Foods illustrates that the way the media portrays an organization can be a conduit to restoring and generating public trust.

In the language of business, trust can be measured by what a person purchases or supports. When I asked Scott McCain, "How do you measure trust?" he said, "market share." In December 2009, it was reported that Maple Leaf returned to profitability, its brand share recovered, its reputation was restored, and top line sales numbers returned to previous levels.

Scott McCain of Maple Leaf Foods recalled the 2008 listeria outbreak and crisis. "It was clearly a landmark crisis, one that tested and challenged trust. It was a very serious breach of trust.

CASE STUDY

We understand the importance of trust at Maple Leaf Foods. There are three things: being open and transparent, we took accountability, no one got fired, and we didn't blame it on the CFIA inspectors. In fact Michael said, 'the buck stops here'. And, we communicated with the public early, on site and we talked to everyone."

Highlights of Case

- Media plays important role in rebuilding trust for companies in a crisis
- We look to leaders to be responsible and accountable
- A sincere, empathetic, compassionate apology rebuilds trust
- Consistent and frequent communications
- Transference of trust through comparisons and third party credible sources
- Company values act as guideline for decision making

Conclusion

You Have to Earn Trust

I f you've read this far, you know there is nothing magic about trust. Trust isn't something endowed by a wise God or conferred on those who haven't earned it simply for their good intentions. Universities don't award degrees in Trust Studies and perhaps unfortunately, trust is not on the curriculum of MBA programs.

Trust is not something you can manufacture or engineer. You either earn it or you don't, and you don't earn it by accident. It's hard work to earn trust, and a concentrated, long-term effort is required to sustain it. The research backs this up. It demonstrates that organizations have to be deliberate and consistent to earn and maintain public and customer trust. It shows that successful organizations operate with organizational values or a code of conduct that embraces trust as a central animating principle.

All participant organizations in the research of this book had values or a code of conduct and many published them. Cascading from organizational values is a combination of behaviours, characteristics and competencies along with activities, interactions and communication practices that engender trust with the public.

I have been in the trust business for my entire career. I have mixed academic research with direct business experience and know that my sense of what was true has been proven over and over again; organizations with high trust outperform those with low trust. The Eight Principles are at the heart of a customer's decision to trust your company. The companies and the leaders that have high trust with their customers, suppliers, employees and stakeholders, apply all of the principles.

There are countless benefits to establishing and protecting trust equity with your external publics, including a strong brand and reputation, successful employee recruitment and retention, repeat business, more opportunities and referrals, and customer commitment and loyalty. Trust allows organizations to take risks and be more creative. With trust, you do not have to be continually checking facts, proving yourself and providing references. Trust enables difficult and honest conversations to take place when they are needed. An atmosphere of trust helps avoid difficult conversations with customers when relationships are strained or damaged. Trust allows organizations to command a premium and to gain market share.

Trust is the easiest way to build loyalty with your customers and external stakeholders — whether they are guests, journalists, shareholders, patients, policy holders, subscribers, members, clients, students, community groups or stakeholders.

All participants in our research stated that trust was important to their organization. Trust is critical, foundational, implicit and strategic. During times of crisis, whether through a mistake or a major breach of public confidence, trust becomes critical to success, in some cases even to survival.

Highly trusted employees can preserve and protect a customer's trust and commitment during difficult times created by management policies that appear contrary to the customers' best interests. External factors in your business or service can also cause strain on trusting relationships and they have to be managed. Trusted employees can do that.

The responsibility for creating trust is dichotomous; it lies with the senior staff, and ultimately it is the CEO's responsibility to set the tone, the strategy and the operational parameters that create trust. Then it's up to the front line staff to execute. It is everyone's responsibility to create trust. Some experts say you can't change peoples' attitudes, only their behaviour. Yet creating an atmosphere of trust creates the conditions for attitudinal change, which leads directly to behavioral change, from the corner office to the shop floor.

The better understanding an organization has of trust internally, the deeper trust it can generate externally. If trust is deemed foundational and implicit, generating it with the external public will be more likely to succeed. As one of my seminar participants said, trust is not as deliberate and explicit as it should be.

In the final analysis, every organization has a responsibility to itself and its customers and clients to build, strengthen and protect relationships of trust. With the Client Trust Index™, it can be managed the same way productivity, efficiency and input costs can be managed. An organization's success or failure to manage trust will show up on its bottom line, where it could mean the difference between profit and loss, success and failure. Learn to build and protect trust. The stakes are too high to do anything less.

Index

PAGE

Acadian Seaplants 132
Adams, Christine 287
Agvent, Greg 12, 184, 239
Alston, David 237, 238
Amabile, Teresa 178
Ambassatours GrayLine 185, 210
Ambir 31
American Express 110
Aquinas, Thomas 130, 131
Arab, Mary Dable 76-82
Are you Listening? 88
Aristotle 130, 131, 171
AT&T 110
Athos, Anthony 36
Badaracco, Joseph L. 161
Baker, Susan C. 95
Balanced Score Card Step-by-Step 181, 182
Barber, Bernard 29
Baylor University 3
Bell Canada 21, 110, 210
Bentham, Jeremy 130
Bhide, Amar 122
Bieron, Brian 244-245
Bird Construction 161
BMW 216
Bonhoeffer, Dietrich 131
Boston Consulting Group 13
Bowles, Camilla Parker 17
British Petroleum (BP) 173, 174
British Royal Family 16
Bromiley, Philip 36
Bronken, Steven 191
Brooks Kimmel, Barbara 7
Brunswick News 136
Brydon, Bill 102, 103
Buddhist Eightfold Path 130

  PAGE

Building Trust With Customers: A Workbook 269
Burke, James E. 173
Burke, Lisa 198-202
Business Development Bank of Canada (BDC) 132, 210
Business Newsmaker of The Year 288
Buss, David 94
Butler, John 284
Campbell, Dennis 185, 210
Canada Bread 281
Canada's Most Admired Corporate Cultures 1
Canadian Food Inspection Agency . . . . ii, 278, 279
Canadian Journal of Communication 35
Canadian Medical Association (CMA) 215, 216
Canadian Press 288
Canadian Public Reations Society(CPRS) 131
Cavanagh, Ian 31
CBC News 284, 288, 290
CFIA 291
Cheng, Raymond 14
Christakis, Nicholas 171
Christian Ten Commandments 130
Churchill, Winston 130, 168
Claremont Graduate University 94
Clark, Joe 180
Cleere, Poppy Rose 243
Clemson University 284
Cléroux, Pierre 210
Client Trust Index™ . . . . vi, 5, 25, 27, 39, 41, 43, 139, 154, 166,
. . . . 182, 183, 190, 205, 206, 208, 234, 295
CNN 12, 56, 184, 239
Coca-Cola Company 221,222
Coke 222
Commisionaires Nova Scotia 103
Commissionaires Canada 57
Computer Sciences Corporation 98
Connected: The Suprising Power of Our Social Networks
    and How They Shape our Lives 171
Corporate Integrity Monitor viii
Costco Wholesale 4, 5, 110, 156, 166
Covey, Stephen 92

PAGE

Cox and Palmer 56
Cox Communications 56
Creating A High Trust Organization 195
CSX Corporation. 220
Cuddy, Amy. 48, 127
Culture Shift in Advanced Industrial Society 250
Cummings, Larry 36
CUSUGA 98
Daily Mail 20
Dalhousie University 37
Danko, William 70
Davis, James. 3
Davison, Janet 284
Dealing With An Angry Public 250
Deepwater Horizon 173
DeGeneres, Ellen 97
Dell. 110
Dirks, Kurt 3
Disney 11, 80, 230
Drucker, Peter. vi,31, 36, 241
Duckworth, Angela Lee. 196
Duhe, Sandra C. 91
Duhigg, Charles xi
Durkheim, Emile 165
eBay 244-246
Economist Magazine 220
Edelman. . . . . ix, 90, 122, 165, 166
Edelman Trust Barometer. . . . . ix, 12, 61, 117, 167, 234, 236, 237, 250, 262
Edelman, Richard. 241
Emerson, Ralph Waldo 189
EY Beacon Institue. 10
EY Canada. 31
F1 Financial Training Services 100, 262
Facebook 110, 233, 265, 287
Facetime. 223
FACTS® Framework viii
Fairholm, Gilbert W. 4, 110
Fast Company Magazine. 97
Feeley, John 215
Ferguson, Sarah 17

PAGE

Field, Patrick 250
Flavelle, Dana 283
Forbes. 237, 244
Fordham University 4
Fort McMurray. 161
Fortune. 40, 41
Fortune Magazine . . . . ix, 262
Four Seasons Hotels and Resorts 55, 132, 165, 166, 179, 180
Fowler, James. 171
Franklin, Benjamin. 121, 145, 180
Garbarro, John 36
General Electric 110
Gerstner, Lou 6
Gladwell, Malcolm. 205
Globe and Mail. 289
Golden Rule 170
Goodman, Ronald 173
Google . . . . xi, 11, 12, 138, 218
Google 2015 Zero Moment of Truth Study 138
Googlers. 11
Grant Thornton 166
Great Place to Work. ix
Grit: The Power of Passion and Preserverance 196
Gustavson Brand Trust Index 1, 4, 147
Hanson, William 22
Harris, Colleen 19
Harvard 88, 161
Harvard Business Review 5, 10, 88, 122, 180
Harvard University 48
Health Canada ii
Hello Magazine Canada 19
Helstab, Susan 132, 165, 180
Henry, Chris 166
HMV. 243
Holiday Inn 224
House of Windsor 16
How Google Works 11
Huawei Technologies. 13
Hurley, Robert 4, 36

PAGE

IBM 6, 110, 198-202
Ikea...228
Image at the Top: Crisis and Renaissance in Corporate Leadereship 173
Inglehart, Ronald 250
Instagram...265
Interaction Associates ix
International Communication Association.............................35, 95
Introhive 237,238
Irving, Jamie...136
Irving Oil..228
Jobs, Steve 107
Johnson and Johnson..173, 174, 290
Jones, Jeanette 286
Joseph Brant Hospital ii
JSM Capital Corp...121
Kant, Immanuel 131, 171
Karp, Harvey..101
Kimmel, Barbara Brooks 7
Knight, Phil..196, 225
Kohltech University 191
Kohltech Windows and Entrance Systems............................117, 190
Kramer, Steven 178
Krishnamurti, Jiddu..89
Kushniryk, Alla..37
L.L. Bean..156, 157, 166
Lady Diana 17
Lamorte, Ben..182
Leadership and the Culture of Trust...................................110
Leisureworld Senior Care ii
Lewis, David J. 29
Line-of-Sight...180
Linguistic Model of Patient Participation in Care..........................95
LinkedIn 13, 138, 265
Listening to People..88
Listeria..279, 281, 290
Listeriosis..i
London Olympics..20
Luhmann, Niklas 29
Lululemon Athletica 224

PAGE

Maclean's Magazine 20
Managing in the Gray 161
Maple Leaf Foods. . . . . ii, iii, 31, 132, 168, 210, 278-291
Mayer, Roger 3
McCain, Michael . . . . iii, 168, 282 - 291
McCain, Scott. 31, 121, 210, 285, 290
McCain Foods. 56, 121, 210, 211
McCombs, Max 280
McDelivery 230
McDonald's. 230, 231
McDonald's Boombox. 231
McGee, Jim 13
McHappy Day 230
McKinsey & Company 155
McLuhan, Marshall 233
Men, Linjuan Rita 235
Mercedes Benz 179
Merrill, David W.. . . . . 72, 73
Microsoft. 89
Middletown, Catherine (Kate). 16-21
Mill, John Stuart. 130
Mitchell, Jason. 88
MOMA 12
Mount Saint Vincent University 37, 169
MTS Allstream 210
National University of Singapore. 3
NBC Today. 19
Netflix 20
New York Times. . . . . xi, 220
New York University 3
Nichols, Ralph G.. . . . . 88, 89
Nike 179, 196, 225, 226
Niven, Paul 181,182
NYSE. 37, 40, 42
O'Gorman, Ned 131
Objectives Key Results (OKR) 11, 12, 182
Ocean Spray 110
Olive, David. 121, 122
Olympics 22
Omidyar, Pierre 244

PAGE

Onalytica 201
OralB 110
Orange Lake Resorts 13, 224
Oreo 110
Outliers 206
Oxford University 280
Parker Bowles, Camilla 17
Pelley, Kevin 190
Pemberton, John S.. 221
People Magazine. 19, 56
Personal Styles and Effective Performance 73
Pfeffer, Jeffrey 180
Pinterest. 265
Powell, Colin. vii
Powell, Douglas 283
PR in Canada 287
Prana Business 180
Presence: Bringing Your Boldest Self to Your Biggest Challenges. 122
Prince Andrew 17
Prince Charles. 17
Prince William . . . . 16 - 21
Project Aristotle xi
Public Health Authority of Canada. ii
Public Relations Society of America (PRSA) 131
Purdue University. 3
Queen Elizabeth. 18, 20, 21
Radian 6. 238
Reagan, Ronald. 112
Reid, Roger 72, 73
Robertson, Dean. 121
Rolls Royce Phantom VI. 19
Rometty, Ginni 200, 201
Ronald McDonald House. 230
Rosenburg, Jonathan 11, 12
Royal Canadian Mounted Police (RCMP). 102
Ruch, Richard 173
Russell Investment Report 262
S&P 500 42
Safety Net Access. 191
Salesforce. 238

PAGE

Sam's Club 5
Schmidt, Eric 11, 12
Schoorman, David 3
Schultz, Howard. 226
Scotiabank. . . . . 76 - 82
Scott, Charlie 282
Shaw, Donald 280
Shockley-Zalaback, Pamela 36
Shoe Dog. 196, 226
Simon, Alyssa 37
Sinek, Simon. 10
Six, Frederique 195
Skype 223
Snapchat 141, 223, 240, 265
Social Media Magazine 238
SOCIAL STYLE Model™ 73
Social Style Theory 73
Socratic method 170
SolutionInc 130, 142, 143
Sopranos 53
Sorge, Arndt 195
Source 210
SoZo Solutions 14
Special Olympics 139
Speedy Muffler 153, 154
Spencer, Diana 17
Standard and Poor (S&P). viii
Standford Business School 180
Stanley, Thomas 70
Starbucks. 78, 136, 226
Start With Why 10
Stevens, Leonard A. 88, 89
Stevenson, Howard H. 122
Success Through Trust 109
Sundararajan, Binod. 37
Susskind, Lawrence 250
Symposium on ASIA-USA Partnership Opportunities (SAUPO) 13, 244
Sztompka, Piotr 191
Takata Corporation. 121
Tamir, Diana 88

PAGE

Tan, Hoon Hwee 3
TED talks 99
Ted X talk 50
Telegraph 19, 89
Temkin Group's Trust Ratings 4
The Crown 20
The Gaurdian 283
The Happiest Toddler on the Block 101
The Logic and Limits of Trust 29
The Progress Principle: Using Small Wins to Ignite Joy, Engagement,
  and Creativity at Work 178
The Millionaire Next Door 70
The Ritz Carleton 80
The Shaw Group 56, 121, 132
The Weather Company 199
Thomson Reuters 13
Tim Horton Children's Foundation 148
Tim Hortons 136, 147, 148, 225
Toronto Public Health i
Toronto Star 121, 283, 284
Trust Across America . . . . viii, 7, 192, 220
Trust and Power 29
Trust as a Social Reality 29
Trust: A Sociological Theory 191
Tsai, Wan-Hsiu Sunny 235
Tufts University 94
Tulk, Heather 31, 210
Twitter 110, 238, 243, 265, 287
Tylenol 173, 290
Uber 78
UberEATS 230
United Airlines vii
United Nations 226
University of California, Berkley Greater Good Science Center 94
University of Miami 235
University of Minnesota 88
University of North Carolina 280
University of Notre Dame 3
University of Pennsylvania 196
University of Richmond 4

PAGE

University of Texas 280
UPS 58
Utilitarians 130
Vimeo. 110
Virgin America 98
Volkswagen vii
Wal-mart 110, 156, 218
Wall Street Journal. 132, 214
Watson, Bernadette 95
Watson, Leon 89
Weigert, Andrew 29
Weight Watchers 10
WestJet. 1,2, 110
Wheeler, John 198
Who Says Elephants Can't Dance? Inside IBM's Historic Turnaround. 6
Whole Foods. 70
Willingness to Communicate Model. 95
Wilson Fuels 56
Wilson, Kemmons 224
Yelp. 138
Youtube . . . . vii, 238, 281, 283, 287
Zak, Paul 94
Zand, Dale 3
Zappos. 80
Zoom 214, 223
Zuckerberg, Mark 233

Additional Information

The Client Trust Index™ - Market and Customer Research

The Client Trust Index™ is a proprietary system to measure client trust as a key performance indicator. It offers a quantifiable Trust Equity score. It gives executives a view into the organization's ability to execute on its strategy from the customers point of view. It is a reliable predictor of future success. Oftentimes, The Client Trust Index™ reveals hidden vulnerabilities and insights. These insights enable you to develop a strategy to put your business ahead of the competition.

For more information visit **www.SuccessThroughTrust.com**

Additional Information

Becoming a Trusted Advisor Program

A 12-module online certificate program which leverages evidence based methodologies and the science of how clients decide to trust.

Created to provide critical support to professionals and managers on their way to becoming leaders and trusted advisors, this program is designed specifically for organizations to deepen and transform relationships and improve customer experiences.

Key Takeaways:

+ Discover how customers decide to trust
+ Understand the trust levers that motivate customers
+ Identify ways to create customer value
+ Examine how using the language of trust affects your customers
+ Develop a trusted advisor intuition and mindset that give you the tools and confidence to succeed.

The self - paced program includes:

+ Practical strategies to strengthen relationships
+ Tips, tools and tactics, including specific phrases to incorporate that deepen client relationships
+ A workbook, a personalized coaching call and online access to answer questions or recommend.

For more information please visit **www.SuccessThroughTrust.com**

Let's Continue the Conversation...

My goal is that this book not be the end of the conversation about trust but the beginning. I am interested in hearing your stories of how you and your organization are building, managing and protecting trust.

I encourage you to share your experiences with your friends and colleagues and discuss how having a customer centric trust culture is the most critical asset and competitive differentiator.

Please feel free to connect with me on LinkedIn at https://www.linkedin.com/in/nataliedoyleoldfield/ or email me directly at NOldfield@SuccessThroughTrust.com